SEX ABUSE HYSTERIA
SALEM WITCH
TRIALS REVISITED

SEX ABUSE HYSTERIA

SALEM WITCH TRIALS REVISITED

Richard A. Gardner, M.D.

Clinical Professor of Child Psychiatry
Columbia University
College of Physicians and Surgeons

Creative Therapeutics,
155 County Road, Cresskill, New Jersey 07626-0317

Library of Congress Cataloging-in-Publication Data

Gardner, Richard A.
    Sex abuse hysteria : Salem witch trials revisited / Richard A.
Gardner
        p.   cm.
    Includes bibliographical references and indexes.
    ISBN 0-933812-22-1
    1. Child molesting—United States.   2. Child molesting—United
States—Investigation.   3. Interviewing in child abuse—United
States.   I. Title.
HQ72.U53G37   1990
362.7'6—dc20   90-20218
                                                                    CIP

PRINTED IN THE UNITED STATES OF AMERICA
10 9 8 7 6 5 4 3 2

To my
new grandaughter
Anna Lauren Gardner

Welcome to the world!
May you enjoy long life,
good health, and an ample share of the
happiness that life can provide.

I have found the missing link between
the higher ape and civilized man: It is we.

Konrad Lorenz

This book derives from my experiences in child custody litigation over the last 25 years. In the early 1980s, in the context of such litigation, I began seeing a new phenomenon, namely, the use of the sex abuse accusation as a powerful weapon for wreaking vengeance on a hated spouse as well as obtaining court support for quick exclusion (and even incarceration) of a partner. Whereas some of these accusations were true, I was convinced that the vast majority were false—the ubiquity of genuine child sex abuse notwithstanding.

My studies on the criteria for differentiating between true and false sex abuse allegations led me to the nursery school/day-care situation, where I was convinced that the majority of such accusations were false. The same hallmarks of the fabricated allegation which I found in custody disputes were present in the day-care and nursery school situations. It soon became apparent that the false accusation phenomenon was part of a national hysteria, similar to—but far more extensive than—what we witnessed in 1692 at the Salem witch trials. The question then naturally arose: What's going on here? This book is an attempt to deal with this problem. My hope is that it will play a role in answering this question but, more importantly, help those children and adults who have and may yet become the true victims of this hysteria.

Other Books by Richard A. Gardner

The Boys and Girls Book About Divorce

Therapeutic Communication with Children: The Mutual
    Storytelling Technique

Dr. Gardner's Stories About the Real World, Volume I

Dr. Gardner's Stories About the Real World, Volume II

Dr. Gardner's Fairy Tales for Today's Children

Understanding Children: A Parents Guide to Child Rearing

MBD: The Family Book About Minimal Brain Dysfunction

Psychotherapeutic Approaches to the Resistant Child

Psychotherapy with Children of Divorce

Dr. Gardner's Modern Fairy Tales

The Parents Book About Divorce

The Boys and Girls Book About One-Parent Families

The Objective Diagnosis of Minimal Brain Dysfunction

Dorothy and the Lizard of Oz

Dr. Gardner's Fables for Our Times

The Boys and Girls Book About Stepfamilies

Family Evaluation in Child Custody Litigation

Separation Anxiety Disorder: Psychodynamics
    and Psychotherapy

Child Custody Litigation: A Guide for Parents
    and Mental Health Professionals

The Psychotherapeutic Techniques of Richard A. Gardner

Hyperactivity, The So-Called Attention-Deficit Disorder,
    and The Group of MBD Syndromes

The Parental Alienation Syndrome and the Differentiation
    Between Fabricated and Genuine Child Sex Abuse

Psychotherapy with Adolescents

Family Evaluation in Child Custody Mediation, Arbitration,
    and Litigation

The Girls and Boys Book About Good and Bad Behavior

The Parental Alienation Syndrome: A Guide for Mental Health
    and Legal Professionals

Self-Esteem Problems of Children: Psychodynamics and
    Psychotherapy

True and False Accusations of Child Sex Abuse

Conduct Disorders of Children: Psychodynamics and
    Psychotherapy

CONTENTS

ACKNOWLEDGMENTS

I am indebted to Carol Gibbon who dedicated herself to the typing of the original manuscript of this book. I am grateful, also, to Linda Gould and Donna La Tourette for their contributions to the updated versions.

I deeply appreciate the careful and instructive copyediting of Muriel Jorgensen and Frances Dubner. I appreciate, also, the efforts of Robert Tebbenhoff of Lind Graphics for his contributions to the production of the book from the original manuscript to final volume. Brian Baldwin and Eleanor Miller lent their considerable artistic talents to the jacket, adding immeasurably to its attractiveness.

The aforementioned, however, provided end-of-the-line contributions. My deepest debts are to the victims—both child and adult—from whom I have learned most of what is contained herein. The children fall into two categories of victimization: (1) those who were indeed victims of bona fide sex abuse and (2) those who were never sexually abused, but became embroiled in a system that deemed them so and thereby subjected them to a series of interrogations, "validations," and "treatment" which caused formidable and even lifelong psychological damage. My heart goes out to the falsely accused adults, some of whom are incarcerated and most of whom have suffered formidable psychological damage. They too have taught me much. It is my hope that this book will play a role (admittedly small) in protecting other such victims from a similar fate.

THE BASIC SEX ABUSE PROBLEM

During the last decade we have witnessed an enormous expansion of attention to and preoccupation with child sex abuse—especially in the public media. Every day newspapers, magazines, and television bombard us with stories about child sex abuse. It is much more common than we have previously realized, we are told. No family, neighborhood, or school is safe, and we must be ever sensitive to its subtle manifestations in our children and ever vigilant for the sex abusers who lurk everywhere. We are warned that these perpetrators are very skillful and cunning; often they operate under our very noses, and may leave little or no trace of their nefarious acts. We can only wonder what's happening. Is it really true that child sex abuse is as ubiquitous as some claim and that we have blinded ourselves to this terrible menace? Or is most, if not all, of this talk about sex abuse just a hoax, a media phenomenon that is guaranteed to sell newspapers, magazines, and television time to a gullible public?

In this book, I present what I consider to be the psychological and social factors that have been operative in bringing about the recent sex abuse obsession in our society. My comments and conclusions are derived primarily from my own personal experiences in this area, especially from my private practice and my professional involvement in sex abuse litigation as an evaluator and expert

1

witness. My personal experiences in this realm have been extensive. I have been involved directly in forensic psychiatry for approximately 30 years and have spent (as best as I can calculate) more than a thousand hours sitting on witness stands testifying in court. During the last 25 years, I have been actively involved in child custody litigation (resulting in three books on the subject [1982, 1986b, 1989b]). And during the last ten years I have been actively involved in sex abuse litigation (resulting in one book on the subject [1987]). I have worked directly and extensively with *all* the actors in the sex abuse drama: the parents, the so-called "validators," the children, the physicians, the prosecutors, the judges, the lawyers, and the so-called "therapists." I have spent about 1,500 hours reviewing, analyzing, and commenting on their reports. To date I have spent approximately 150 hours reviewing and analyzing the videotaped interviews of the evaluators. And these involvements have not just been in the greater New York City area, where I live and practice. Rather, I have conducted consultations and provided testimony in a dozen states and have lectured to legal and mental health professionals in 20 more. However, these travels have not been one-way experiences in which I have merely provided information to my audiences. Rather, I have gotten significant feedback from them, feedback which has enhanced my knowledge in this realm.

What I am providing here are essentially my story and my understanding of what is going on. Because it is my purpose to present primarily my personal views, there is a paucity of references to other publications, both professional and lay. For every point I make I could have found numerous references in support of my position, as well as numerous references in refutation. In the hysterical atmosphere in which we are living, publications in either camp would not be hard to find. The term *scientific proof* is not applicable to most of the issues discussed here. There are, however, dozens (and probably hundreds) of cases in which there is great dispute regarding whether *legal proof* of sex abuse has been established. Rather than provide myself with the specious buttressing of my position with selective quotations from other sources (each of which could be argued against by a selected quotation from yet another source), I will state here plainly my own opinions on these issues.

Some claim that much of the obsession with child sex abuse is "media hype," or mass hysteria, and that bona fide "proven" child sex abuse is relatively rare. In contrast, others hold that a child who claims to have been sexually abused must be telling the truth. "Children never lie" about such things, they claim, because a child has no direct exposure to information about sexual encounters and therefore if such a description has been provided, it must be valid. "Believe the children" has become the slogan of parents, educators, and prosecutors in many of these cases. Those who claim that many children's allegations of sex abuse are fabrications, distortions, delusions, and/or the result of adult programming are viewed with suspicion and are often vociferously condemned. At this point, I suspect that there are many more individuals who believe that we are indeed dealing with an epidemic of sex abuse than those who believe that the whole problem is being exaggerated by mass hysteria.

As a result of this dispute, many individuals are placed (or have placed themselves) in one of two camps: those who believe that children's allegations are true and those who hold that they are false. But we are not dealing here with an either/or situation. The problem does not simply boil down to the question of whether the majority of children's allegations of sex abuse are true or false. When asking about the likelihood of a sex abuse allegation being true or false, one must ask the question: Which situation are we talking about? In some situations, there is a high likelihood an allegation is true; in others, there is a very low likelihood the allegation is valid. Sex abuse allegations that arise in the intrafamilial situation have a high likelihood of being valid. Incest is probably quite common, especially father (or stepfather)-daughter (or stepdaughter) relations. Obviously, it would be impossible to obtain accurate statistics on this subject, but I believe that there is strong evidence to support the conclusion that it is a widespread phenomenon and probably has a longstanding history—dating back to the birth of mankind.

In contrast, sex abuse allegations made in the context of child custody disputes (especially those that are litigated viciously) have a high likelihood of being false. An accusation of sex abuse can be a very effective method of wreaking vengeance on a hated spouse and will certainly speed up the court's dealing with the case. The accusation may result in immediate cessation of visitation by the accused, can literally ruin the career of a hated spouse, and can cause other devastating psychological sequelae and traumas. Accordingly, it is a tempting weapon to use in a bitter child custody dispute. I am not claiming that bona fide child sex abuse cannot occur in the context of a child custody dispute; I am only saying that such allegations are more likely to be false than true—considering the context in which they arise. Elsewhere (1987, 1988a, 1989a) I have described in detail the criteria that one can utilize to differentiate between fabricated and bona fide sex abuse allegations in the context of custody disputes.

Another situation that has been given significant attention in recent years is the day-care center and nursery school. The McMartin case in California has probably been the best known of these (Carlson, 1990; Nathan, 1990). I believe that the likelihood is that the vast majority of allegations in this category are false, even though many of the accusing children ultimately come to believe that they have been abused (the usual situation). These cases have all the hallmarks of mass hysteria similar to that which took place at the time of the Salem witch trials in 1692 (Mappan, 1980; Richardson, 1983). I will discuss these similarities (and differences) in Chapter Fourteen. It is probably true that child sex abuse is a common phenomenon in boarding schools, orphanages, and other settings in which children live together with adults. I do not believe that child sex abuse resulting from predators lurking in neighborhoods is a common phenomenon, although it certainly does exist.

Accordingly, when talking about the prevalence of child sex abuse, one must be careful to identify the particular setting in which one is speculating about how common the phenomenon is. Otherwise, the question of prevalence becomes meaningless. There are areas of high likelihood of prevalence and there are areas of low likelihood. Residential centers, orphanages, and boarding schools— because they provide the opportunity for ongoing involvement with the child—are high-risk places for child sex abuse. English boarding schools (where the sex abuse has often been associated with the sadomasochistic component) are well known for this phenomenon. I believe that the important principle to consider when predicting the risk is that of the opportunity for the pedophile to have ongoing and prolonged contact with a potential child victim. When this principle is applied to the aforementioned categories, the ostensible disparity of prevalence risks becomes understandable. In the home situation, where a parent has the greatest opportunity for ongoing involvement with the child, there is the greatest risk for child sex abuse. Although parents involved in a child custody dispute also have such opportunities (much more for the primary custodial parent than the visiting parent), the issue of vengeance and potential for exclusion must be given serious consideration when making a determination as to whether or not child sex abuse took place. In contrast, in nursery schools and day-care centers, where the opportunity for ongoing contact with a child alone is very small, the risk of bona fide abuse is low. I am not claiming that there is absolutely no sex abuse in the nursery school and day-care setting. Certainly, pedophiles are likely to be attracted to employment in such settings where they may have the opportunity for sexually abusing children. I am only claiming that the prevalence is low.

Throughout the course of this book I use the common dictionary definition of pedophile, namely, an adult who has a sexual relationship with a child. There are some who confine this term to situations in which the perpetrator is previously unknown to the child and use the term *incest* to refer to the intrafamilial situation. Of course, this is a perfectly acceptable differentiation as long as all parties involved appreciate that this distinction is being made. There are many situations in which it may be very difficult to decide whether the term pedophilia is warranted. This is especially the case when one considers the age-difference factor between the two individuals. The American Psychiatric Association's Diagnostic Manual (*DSM-III-R*) defines pedophilia as a sexual act between a person who is "at least 16 years old with a child . . . generally age 13 or younger." Furthermore, there must be at least a five-year age difference between the perpetrator and the child. However, the term would not be applicable if "a late adolescent was involved in an ongoing sexual relationship with a 12- or 13-year-old." There are obvious difficulties with this definition. For example, if there is a four-and-a-half-year age difference between the two people, then the perpetrator would not be considered a pedophile. Also, a 15-1/2-year-old who has a sexual encounter with a four-year-old would not be considered a pedophile. Legal definitions of pedophilia vary from state to state and are even more complex and mind-boggling. Furthermore, the stringency with which they are implemented varies, and the final decision usually relates more to the emotions of the judge and jury than strict adherence to the legal definition that is ostensibly being subscribed to. Although the legal and psychiatric definitions do not generally distinguish between relatives and nonrelatives, strangers are usually dealt with much more punitively than those who are family members. And fathers and stepfathers are dealt with much more punitively than siblings.

My focus in this book is on the false sex abuse allegations that are made in the context of day-care centers and nursery schools. To a lesser extent, I deal with false sex abuse allegations that occur in the context of child custody disputes. Although there are some differences in the ways in which these allegations originate, they share an amazing similarity with regard to the progressive development of the allegations, from plausible to implausible—from reasonable to preposterous, to impossible. In fact, it is the preposterous and even impossible elements that are important clues to their being false.

Throughout this book I will use the word *false* to cover the wide variety of allegations that have no basis in reality. There are times when the child and/or accuser are consciously fabricating. They know quite well that the accusation has no basis in reality, and they are consciously aware that they are lying. Another category of false accusation is the one in which there is only minimal evidence for abuse and the individual has some psychological need to elaborate, exaggerate, and transform the scintilla of possible evidence into the belief that abuse actually occurred. Another category of false accusation involves the projection of one's own unacceptable sexual impulses onto an innocent party. The other party, then, becomes the perpetrator and/or victim. This is one of the central elements in prejudice and, when severe, the term *delusion* is applicable. Last, there is the category of individuals who begin with a fabrication and then come to believe their lies. I will use the term *false allegation* to refer to all of these types of allegations. They share in common the basic fact that the abuse never took place.

It is important for the reader to appreciate that there is no simple explanation for the development and entrenchment of children's false sex abuse allegations. Children's false sex abuse allegations have played a central role in the sex abuse hysteria we have witnessed in the last decade. Many factors are involved, and they interact with one another. I describe here what I consider to be the primary factors and delineate what I consider to be the mechanisms by which each of these factors operates.

Last, I wish to emphasize that I fully appreciate that genuine sex abuse of children is widespread and the vast majority of sex abuse allegations of children (from *all* of the aforementioned categories combined) are likely to be justified (perhaps 95% or more). The focus of this book, however, is on the false accusations for which there is absolutely no basis in reality. Although the latter represents only a small fraction of the former, the results of such false accusations are tragic for both the alleged victims and accused perpetrators. Children in these cases become victims of the system designed to assess the validity of the accusation and the innocents so accused become the victims of the false accusations. It is my hope that this book will not only elucidate the factors operative in bringing about such a wave of victimization but play a role in reversing this tragic phenomenon.

2

THE NORMAL FANTASIES
OF CHILDHOOD

Sigmund Freud (1905) referred to children as "polymorphous perverse." I am in full agreement with Freud on this point. Children normally exhibit just about any kind of sexual behavior imaginable: heterosexual, homosexual, bisexual, and autosexual. Infants have no problem caressing any part of anyone's body, whether it be a private part or a public part. And they have absolutely no concern for the gender of the possessor of the target part. Nor do they concern themselves with that person's sexual orientation. They will put into their mouths any object that will fit, whether it be their own or anyone else's. They touch all parts of their own bodies, and attempt to touch all parts of other people's bodies. In short, they touch, suck, insert, smell, and feel all the parts of their own as well as other human beings and make no particular discriminations regarding the age, sex, or relationship to them of the object of their "sexual" advances. Each society has its own list (most often quite specific) regarding which types of sexual behavior are acceptable and which are prohibited. Generally, parents provide this information in the early years of the child's life and react quite strongly when the child attempts to engage in one of the unacceptable forms of sexual behavior, that is, unacceptable in accordance with the consensus of individuals in the particular society in which the child has been born.

In our society we generally attempt to lead the child down the heterosexual track, but even here we suppress heterosexual behaviors to varying degrees up until the time of marriage and even afterward. Even in the marital bed most subscribe to a particular "list" of behaviors that are acceptable, and may exhibit strong revulsion when a spouse requests a sexual encounter that is not on the "list." But even when social suppression and repression have been successful (regarding overt behavior), residua of the early primitive polymorphous perversity persist. These suppressed impulses can be gratified in fantasy, symbolism, or vicariously by thinking about others who engage in these activities. Psychiatrists refer to those whose primary orientation is a residuum of the unacceptable and/or atypical as psychopathological or symptomatic. The man in the street will refer to these individuals as perverted. Many years ago, during my residency training, I came to this conclusion: We label as perverts those who engage in sexual behaviors that we personally find disgusting. Because their behavior disgusts us, it is probable that we are suppressing and/or repressing our own unconscious desires to engage in the very behavior we so detest.

Some examples: A three-year-old boy is playing with his penis. Many parents would hold that masturbation is a perfectly natural act, but tell the child that what he is doing is a personal matter and should not be done in front of other people. The child might also be told that if he wishes to engage in that behavior, he should do so in the privacy of his own room. This is the kind of comment that many educated parents would tell their children at this time. However, even this comment communicates certain socially induced restrictions and prohibitions. The boy would not be told that it is improper in public to stick his finger in his ear, to scratch his head, or to rub his knee. It is just the genital area that requires seclusion if there is to be any kind of hand contact. Other parents might react differently. Some would do everything possible to stop the child from engaging in the activity. They might use physical restraints (quite common in the late nineteenth century) or threaten the boy that they will take him to the doctor and have his penis cut off. (This is what happened to Freud's famous patient, Little Hans [Freud, 1909].) The first child grows up "normal" with regard to masturbation, confining himself to doing it only in private places and not publicly. The second child might develop inhibitions in this area and even "castration anxiety," as did Little Hans.

A little girl rubs her vulva and clitoris and then enjoys smelling the vaginal secretions on her fingers. Again, there are a wide variety of parental responses. However, in our society, even those who approve of masturbation might not approve of the olfactory sequela. Because cunnilingus is generally acceptable behavior in male/female heterosexuality (in our society at this time), it is acceptable for men to enjoy smelling these female secretions—but not women. We have a double standard here—a double standard that may contribute to a woman's feeling of disgust over the odors of her own genitals.

It is acceptable for male and female infants to enjoy sucking breasts. After the weaning period, children learn that breast sucking is only for infants. Men are allowed to engage in this "infantile" behavior as part of normal foreplay, but women who maintain a desire for such activity might be labeled as having "lesbianic tendencies"—without any connotation that this might be part of the normal female repertoire.

A three-year-old girl and her four-year-old brother are taking a shower with their father. In the course of the frolicking, each child might entertain a transient fantasy of putting the father's penis in his (her) mouth. Considering the relative heights of the three individuals, and considering the proximity of the children's mouths to the father's penis under these circumstances, it is not surprising that such a fantasy might enter each of the children's minds. It might even be expressed in the form of the children's saying laughingly, "I'm going to bite off your penis." Being so close at the time of their lives when they insert everything in sight into their mouths, it is not surprising that this fellatio fantasy is evoked in the shower. In this setting, they may both learn that this is unacceptable behavior. However, residua of these fantasies and drives may very well persist into adult life. The woman is freer to express these in a heterosexual encounter with a man (who is likely to derive great pleasure from the act). However, the boy who exhibits a continued interest in such behavior will at best be considered to have "homosexual tendencies" and may very well be considered a homosexual. Again, we see the very specific selection process and the special gender requirements for each of the sexes.

Anal functions are probably subjected to the most vigorous prohibitions. It was acceptable to say (under certain very restricted and specific circumstances) that one has had a good bowel movement and that one has enjoyed a sense of relief and pleasure. Men (especially adolescent boys) in our society are much freer to make such comments than women, but I cannot imagine that women do not enjoy the same sensations. In old age homes, however, there appears to be gender-blind permissiveness with regard to a discussion of this topic. Anal stimulation in sexual encounters, however, is generally frowned upon and is viewed as "disgusting" and "perverted." Infants, before they have learned about these social attitudes, have no problem playing with their (or anyone else's) anus or feces—smelling, licking, and even putting such waste in their mouths.

Our attitudes toward flatus is a good example of the power of the social influence on the selective process. It is reasonable to assume that the odor of flatus is approximately the same for all individuals (within a relatively narrow range). The metabolic processes that result in the formation of these gases is quite similar in all physically healthy human beings. Yet, we generally are disgusted by the flatus of other people, but not by our own. We are generally disgusted with the sounds that other people emit when they pass gas, but we do not feel such revulsion when we ourselves create identical sounds. And this distinction (the reader will please excuse this very subtle pun) is socially learned.

My main point, for the purposes of this book, is that the *normal* child exhibits a wide variety of sexual fantasies and behaviors, many of which would be labeled as "sick" or "perverted" if exhibited by adults. I am not claiming that every child fantasizes about every type of sexual activity in the human repertoire. Each child is likely to have a "favorite" list of sexual activities that provide interest and pleasure. Those who claim that children who verbalize such fantasies or exhibit such behaviors could not have had any actual experiences in these areas have little understanding (or memory) of normal child sexuality. Those who have gone further and have considered such manifestations as "proof" that a child has been sexually abused have caused many truly innocent individuals an enormous amount of harm, even to the point of long prison sentences.

3

SEX ABUSE PREVENTION PROGRAMS

In the normal, healthy child the aforementioned sexual thoughts and activities occupy a relatively minor part of the child's life. The biological procreative urges are weak, the social opportunities for gratification limited, and the parental discouragement is effective in bringing about suppression and repression of these impulses. And the desire to maintain the affection of significant figures (parents, teachers, and their surrogates) and to avoid alienating these important figures plays an important role in the processes that relegate these drives to preconscious and unconscious levels of awareness. However, there are certain environmental exposures that are likely to enhance a child's sexual preoccupations, and one of these is the sex abuse prevention program. During the last decade, with the burgeoning attention to sex abuse, schools everywhere have set up special programs designed to help children protect themselves from sex abuse. I question the effectiveness of such programs. It is very difficult to say whether or not they have been successful in their aim of reducing the sexual abuse of children. But even if they have been successful in this regard, there is no question that they do "plant seeds" and engender in the child's mind sexual fantasies that may not previously have been in the child's repertoire. Traditionally, these programs confront children with information about "good touches" and "bad touches." Good touches involve touching the child in various places but not, obviously, in the genital or anal areas. Bad touches, obviously, relate to touches in these "prohibited" areas. In the context of such discussion, fantasies are engendered about various people—including family members—who might be involved in such touching. One cannot visualize being touched in a "bad" place without visualizing at least the hand and generally the rest of the body of the toucher. The potential toucher may be someone familiar with the child or someone who is not familiar.

Generally, these programs, in order to protect the child from sex abuse from family as well as nonfamily members, include the wide variety of potential perpetrators. Fears are thereby engendered in the child, fears of both family and nonfamily members. The programs, if "successful," are likely to create a state of vigilance in which the child is encouraged to be ever on the lookout for a sex abuse perpetrator. No person is free from suspicion: father, uncles, grandfathers, and certainly strangers in the street. With some justification, females are generally depicted as being less likely suspects than males. These programs can engender in a child the feeling that it is dangerous business to be alone in a room with a relative and that a sex abuser may be lurking in every shadow, behind every tree, and around every corner.

The programs probably engender various kinds of confusion in most children. How does the child distinguish between innocent hugs and kisses from those that may escalate into sex abuse. Where does the child draw the line? Children cannot possibly make the subtle distinctions that are often necessary for such discriminations. And what about bathing? Those who formulate such programs have difficulty with the bathing issue. Should any kind of adult bathing along with a child be proscribed? If not, what should be the upper age limit for such bathing? And what about washing? Normally, every good parent washes the child's crotch area. Such washing must inevitably involve a certain amount of contact with erogenous zones. How can the child learn to differentiate between the normal amount of pleasure that such stimulation provides and that degree which could justifiably be called sex abuse. Should the parent just skip from the bellybutton to the knees and thereby avoid any problem in this department? Such confusion can extend to the message that the child has the right to say no. This is a frequently emphasized part of such programs. There are children who will use this advice as justification for saying no to their parents in response to the wide variety of requests, demands, and disciplinary measures used in the home. Further confusion is created by the child's being told that it is all right for parents and doctors to touch private parts, but not all right for others to touch them.

In addition to programs provided in schools, children now have available to them audiotapes, as well as reading and coloring books, in which such programs are presented. This further intensifies the seed-planting phenomenon, the confusion, the heightened state of vigilance, and the tension and anxieties promulgated by the school programs.

I believe that some of the people who are involved in such programs are well meaning and genuinely believe that they are providing a public service by helping protect children from sex abuse. They argue that the program can discourage a potential sex abuser because of his knowledge that the child has been instructed properly and will thereby be less likely to be receptive and more likely to report the abuser to adult authorities. I believe that some who are involved in these programs have a hidden agenda in the psychopathological realm. They are overly zealous, even to the point of fanaticism. These are the people who have dedicated themselves to "stamping out" sex abuse, and the widespread use of school programs is one step toward this noble goal. Many involved in such programs obtain vicarious gratification from their involvement. They, like the rest of us, have primitive and infantile sexual drives that need socially acceptable release and gratification. The program provides a useful vehicle for the satisfaction for such impulses. Each time they envision an adult sexually abusing a child, they are provided with vicarious gratification of their own pedophilic impulses. They can protect themselves from the knowledge that their motives are psychopathological with the rationalization that theirs is indeed a worthy cause.

Although one could argue that these programs have indeed contributed to the prevention of child sex abuse, the identification of some sex abusers, and the protection of those children who were actually being abused (or on the verge of being so), there is no question that much harm has been done as well via the churning up and promulgating of sexual fantasies and the contribution thereby that they make to the false sex abuse phenomenon. My own belief is that they have done more harm than good, that the number of children who have benefited from such programs is small compared to the number of children who have been psychologically trauma- tized by them. Goleman (1990) describes some of the research being done at this time in this area and Krivacska (1989) provides a comprehensive statement on the subject.

4

THE UBIQUITY OF ENVIRONMENTAL SEXUAL STIMULI

The ubiquity of environmental sexual stimuli is playing a role in the epidemic of false sex abuse allegations that we have witnessed in the last decade. In the last 15 to 20 years we have experienced progressive relaxation of the restrictions that were previously placed on the public exposure of sexually explicit material. In the early days of movies, sexual material was strictly censored. People would flock to movie houses to be titillated by famous movie stars kissing (*always* with closed mouths). Even the mildest profanities were prohibited. In 1939, Clark Gable's use of the word "damn" in *Gone With The Wind* was considered scandalous by many, but people flocked to the box office—in part to witness for themselves this titillating departure from the official norms.

In retrospect all this seems quaint. Now, our R-rated movies use the most prohibited vulgarisms. Many rock singers are obsessed with them. If parents are willing to listen carefully to the lyrics, they will hear just about every profanity commonly used in the English language. And this fare is available on standard television, especially Music Television (MTV). Although many comedians are not permitted to use profanities on standard TV channels, they can present their more vulgar material on cable channels and in theaters and clubs.

19

Today, standard cinema fare allows one to witness sexual acts, the only restriction being that one cannot observe a penis going into a vagina. (Penises and vaginas not involved in the act of copulation are still permissible.) Those interested in viewing this aspect of a sexual encounter can easily find theaters showing X-rated movies or view pornographic home videotapes. Accordingly, both parents and children (the latter often surreptitiously) have their sexual titillation easily available.

People in the cinema serve as our models—whether we like it or not. We generally work on the principle that if it's okay to say it on television, it's okay to say it elsewhere. Accordingly, we have witnessed an enormous relaxation with regard to the acceptability of profanity in private and public places. Adults today use profanities more freely and they serve as models for their children. And they cannot with conviction restrict the use of profanities by their children when they themselves are not "practicing what they preach." When I went to high school in the 1940s, girls who used profanities (a relatively rare occurrence) were generally viewed as being loose in morals and most likely promiscuous. Today, most high school girls in most communities in the United States (I did not say *all*) are quite comfortable using profanities, and those who hesitate to use these words are generally viewed as being somewhat "uptight." The permissiveness in the adult world with regard to the use of profanities filters down to adolescents, and then down to preadolescents, and then down to younger children—even to the point where a profanity may be among a child's first words. In many families, that is considered "cute." There was a time when the nursery school repertoire was generally confined to "pee-pee" and "doo-doo" or words of similar connotation. All that is passé. The nursery school set now speaks about sticking fingers and "pecnics" into "ginas."

One of the effects of all this permissiveness has been ubiquitous titillation. Sexual stimuli bring about hormonal secretions into the bloodstream and genital excitation with a wide range of results, depending upon the individual. A few years ago a mother complained to me that her eight-year-old son and his friend were playing a new game they called "Rape." The game involved the two boys suddenly jumping on their housekeeper (a woman of about 25) with the intent to grab her breasts and stick their fingers into her vagina. In the service of this goal, they would try to rip off her clothes and restrain her arms. The woman had to beat the boys off with her fists and kick them quite strongly before they got the message that she was not going to involve herself in this "game." In the course of these encounters it became apparent to her that both of the boys had erections. On inquiry I learned that the boys were secretly watching the parents' pornographic videotapes, the place where they learned this game. The cure for this problem was the parents placing their videotapes under lock and key. I mentioned this patient's experience because it serves as a good example of the effects on children of their exposure to the sexual stimuli that surround them.

With regard to the containment of sexual urges stimulated by external stimuli, there is a continuum (as is true for most things in this world). At the one end of the continuum are those people with very powerful suppressive (conscious) and repressive (unconscious) psychological mechanisms, with the result that they are able to block from conscious awareness their titillation. However, they may have to resort to the utilization of various complex psychological mechanisms that allow release (symbolically or vicariously) without conscious awareness that pent-up sexual needs are being gratified. At the other end of the continuum are those who are driven to seek every possible sexual gratification because of the bombardment of stimuli that they are continually being exposed to. And children are no exception to this principle. A newborn infant can be brought to orgasm if an adult chooses to masturbate the child (and I am not recommending this practice). Obviously, the greater the intensity of the stimuli, the greater the frequency, the greater the excitation, and the greater the likelihood of acting out. In the world in which we live, the ubiquity of sexual stimuli is causing many children—even those at the highly suppressed end of the continuum—to exhibit sexual interest and excitation. And providing a false sex abuse allegation is one possible—and increasingly available—route for release.

5

THE PARENTAL CONTRIBUTION

One of the factors that has contributed to the epidemic of false sex abuse allegations we have witnessed in the last decade became operative in the context of child custody disputes; it then spread to the nursery school and day-care situation. Child custody disputes have been burgeoning since the late 1960s for a variety of reasons. The passage of no-fault divorce laws made it much easier for people to divorce. The more divorces there are, the more custody disputes there will be. Prior to the 1970s, under the "tender years presumption," mothers were generally considered to be the preferable parent when there was a custody dispute. In the mid-1970s, fathers claimed that the "tender years presumption" was essentially sexist, and it was replaced with the "best interests of the child presumption" wherein custody decisions (by both courts and mental health professionals) were made on the basis of criteria having nothing to do with the gender of the parent, but rather parenting capacity per se. This change resulted in more frequent and even more bitter child custody disputes, its ostensible egalitarianism notwithstanding. In the late 1970s and early 1980s we witnessed an increased popularity of the joint custodial concept. Once again, an increase in parental egalitarianism resulted in an increasing frequency of child custody disputes. Elsewhere (Gardner, 1982,

1986a, 1987, 1989b), I have discussed these phenomena in great detail.

As a result of this burgeoning of child custody disputes, cases take much longer to be brought to trial and the delays have caused considerable frustration and psychopathology (in parents and children). Furthermore, these recent trends have eroded the strength that women had under the protection of the tender years presumption in which they were viewed, because they were women, as being preferable custodial parents. Under the best interests of the child presumption, courts were presumably "sex blind" and parenting capacity was judged basically on parenting ability, regardless of parental gender. In such an atmosphere, a mother's allegation of child sex abuse became a very powerful weapon. It brought about quick action by the courts as well as immediate removal of a hated husband. Of all the accusations that an irate mother could make against her despised husband, a sex abuse allegation proved to be the most devastating. The wrath of the judge was predictably invoked, and immediate cessation of visitation became the order of the day. Pending a plenary hearing (which could take months or even years), the mother could "retrench," strengthen her bonds with the children (uncontaminated by the father's intrusions), and strengthen thereby her position when the case finally came to trial. Predictably, her lawyer would usually agree with her that a more powerful weapon could not be found, and the lawyer did not inquire too deeply into the allegation, lest the lawyer's incredulity contaminate the process. In fact, there were lawyers who were actually encouraging their clients to make such an allegation, knowing all the while that there was absolutely no evidence for it. In the mid-to-late 1980s, in a backlash maneuver, men began accusing their wives of sexually abusing children; however, this retaliatory maneuver has never been widely utilized.

Whereas traditional custody disputes did not receive much attention by the public media (except when celebrities were involved), these cases (for obvious reasons) received significant public attention. They contributed thereby to the plethora of sexual stimuli to which the public was being increasingly exposed. The publicity these cases received played a role in the nursery school and day-care sex abuse phenomena. They are best viewed as one of the catalytic processes that facilitated the epidemic whose origins relate to a wide variety of factors described in this book.

So much for historical development. More important are the psychodynamic factors operative in parents in both of these situations. In both of these situations false allegations of child sex abuse are common. Although there are some points of difference between the child custody dispute and the day-care situation, the major psychological gratifications provided parents in both groups are quite similar. Adults too are "polymorphous perverse." As mentioned, children have to learn which "perversities" are acceptable and which are not to significant adults in their environment. The suppressed and repressed drives press for expression, and a wide variety of psychological mechanisms allow for their release without the individual's being consciously aware that the process is taking place. Here I detail some of the more common mechanisms.

VICARIOUS GRATIFICATION

One such mechanism is *vicarious gratification*. We cannot involve ourselves in sexual encounters with more than a small fraction of all the human beings with whom we might want to have such experiences. While watching a movie star involved in such activity on the screen, we identify with one of the lovers (usually of the same sex) and gratify vicariously our desires for such an encounter ourselves. The same mechanism may be operative in parents' false sex abuse allegations. Each time the accusers make an accusation, they are likely to be forming an internal visual image of the sexual encounter. With each mental replay, the accusers gratify the desire to be engaging in the activities that the perpetrators are involved in in the visual imagery.

The cinema example of the vicarious gratification process is easy for most people to accept. After all, we are normal, healthy heterosexuals, and those people depicted on the screen are also normal, healthy heterosexuals. But the same mechanism holds for visual images of pedophilic sexual encounters. Each time we conjure up a visual image of the child being sexually abused, we gratify vicariously our own pedophilic impulses. Consistent with my agreement with Freud that all infants are polymorphous perverse, I believe that all of us have some pedophilia within us. People with a very strong tendency in this area are more likely to need such visual imagery more frequently and are more likely, therefore, to be willing participants in a false sex abuse allegation. If the need is great, they are willing to "suspend disbelief" and ignore information that might suggest that the alleged perpetrator is indeed innocent. The identification in this image can be with either of the participants, the child or the alleged perpetrator. Identifying with the child allows gratification of one's desire to be the object of the sexual encounter, and identification with the alleged perpetrator allows for gratification of the desire to be the seducer. When one identifies with the "victim" one is basically saying, "I would like him (her) to do that to me." When one identifies with the perpetrator one is basically saying, "I would like to do that with the child." Of course, for the vast majority of people this phenomenon is unconscious. Most people are too guilt ridden over their pedophilic impulses to allow these fantasies direct entry into conscious awareness: thus, the formation of the vicarious gratification mode of release. The impulses are satisfied without the individual feeling guilty or being consciously aware that such impulses reside within himself (herself).

PROJECTION

Another mechanism operative in the false allegation is that of *projection*—by which cognitively and emotionally unacceptable thoughts and feelings are unconsciously rejected and attributed to others. People with excessive guilt or shame over their pedophilic impulses may project out their own desires onto another. It is as if they are saying: "It is not I who would want to sexually molest this child, it is he (she)." In this way unacceptable impulses are gratified, guilt over their release is assuaged, and the individual is left guiltless. The greater the strength of the individual's repressed and unacceptable pedophilic impulses, the greater will be the need for an ever-expanding horde of "pedophiles" to serve as objects for projections. This mechanism is central to prejudice. Typically, the "others" are viewed as more sexually promiscuous, incestuous, perverted, homosexual, homicidal, and prone to the wide variety of perversities that we fine folk do not include in our repertoire of human behaviors.

Projection is a powerful mechanism that is ubiquitous. Most have heard at some time or other anecdotes about people who are looking for "the secret of life"—the one great wisdom under which is encompassed all the meaning of life's experiences. The jokes and/or stories often involve seeking the secret from some guru, often seated in some mountain cave in India or high in the Himalayas. After a long, arduous, circuitous route, during which time the individual(s) may have been exposed to many dangers, the wise man is finally confronted with the question: "What is the secret (or meaning) of life?" Well, I have the answer here for the reader. (Remember, it was I who told it to you.) The secret of life is this: *Life is a Rorschach Test!* Yes, that's it. Life is a Rorschach Test. (The Rorschach is a psychological test in which the patient is shown a series of cards on which there are inkblots. The patient is asked to tell about what he [she] sees therein.) Under this dictum one can subsume all psychological experiences of life. In every experience there is the reality and there is the interpretation that we make of it, depending upon our own psychic structure. There is the Rorschach inkblot, and there is the patient's projection, which gives meaning to the inkblot. There is the external reality, and there is the interpretation we give to it. And there is yet another level here, namely, the *interpretation* the psychologist gives to the patient's projection. This reflects the psychologist's *own* values (whether the projection is "sick" or "healthy") and must also be considered part of the reality. There is the glass of water, and there is our interpretation as to whether it is half empty or half full, or whatever other meaning we want to give to it. The reality then is not simply an external entity. Rather, it is a *combination* of an external entity and the meaning and interpretation that our internal psychic structure gives to it. The two together then determine our thoughts, feelings, and actions. Let us hope that our projections and our interpretations of what is good and bad for our patients will serve them well.

The principle is well demonstrated by the anecdote about the man who is being examined by a psychologist. The following interchange takes place:

> *Psychologist:* I'm going to draw some pictures for you and I'd like you to tell me what comes to mind as you look as each of them. All right, let's do the first. (At this point the psychologist draws two parallel lines on a piece of paper.) Now, look at what you see here and tell me what comes to mind.
>
> *Patient:* Oh that's an easy one, Doc, that's two people and they're having sexual relations.
>
> *Psychologist:* Okay, now I'm going to show you another one. (At this point the psychologist draws two circles, one next to the other.) Now look at this and tell me what comes to your mind.
>
> *Patient:* Doctor, that's another easy one. That's two *fat* people having sex.
>
> *Psychologist:* Okay, now let's try this one. (Now the psychologist draws a rectangle.) What comes to your mind as you look at *this?*
>
> *Patient:* Doc, that's a snap! That's a bed and you're looking down on it. There are two people in there and they are screwing. They're really going at it.
>
> *Psychologist:* Okay now, we're going to try *one more.* (Psychologist now draws a single line in the middle of the page.) So what do you see *here?*
>
> *Patient:* Doctor, you've given me another easy one. That's a fence there. You're looking down on it. There's a guy on one side and a girl on the other. The guy jumps over the fence and he has sex with the girl.
>
> *Psychologist:* You know, you're very much preoccupied with sex.
>
> *Patient:* Me? I'm preoccupied with sex? But you're the one who's showing me all those dirty pictures!

The anecdote demonstrates clearly the power of the projection process. We see in external stimuli what we wish to see in them. The external stimulus is far less important a determinant of what we see than the "eye of the beholder."

Projection is a very valuable defense mechanism because it allows the individual to feel guiltless over the unacceptable impulses that are ever pressing for release. The need for the utilization of projection may be so strong that the individual may have to deny obvious realities that would disprove the allegation. In such cases we refer to the allegation as a delusion and this is central to the paranoid mechanism. Typically, delusions are not dispelled by confrontations with reality. Rather, the "disproof" is interpreted in some way to be just another "proof." For example, if the judge rules that there is absolutely no evidence for sex abuse and that the accuser is either fabricating and/or delusional, the accuser then concludes that the judge is being secretly paid off by the alleged perpetrator—even though the latter may have been left penniless by the litigation.

Delusions are very powerful defense mechanisms. They represent a break with reality and are not generally dispelled by logic, no matter how persuasive and compelling. Confrontations with "proof" that the delusion is a distortion do not generally work. It is for this reason that they are one of the hallmarks of psychosis, a group of disorders in which a break with reality is a central manifestation. Although statistics on this subject would be very difficult to obtain, it is probable that there are many more delusional people than is generally recognized. Not all psychotics are hospitalized; in fact, the vast majority are not. And not all psychotics are recognized as "crazy" by any passerby. Many look "normal," yet they may have isolated areas of psychotic thinking, such as delusions. And there is also the phenomenon that is best described as *mass delusion*. Here, predelusional people, those who are prone to develop psychotic symptoms, take on the delusions of others. This is especially common in the context of mass hysteria situations. Others, not necessarily prepsychotic, may take on delusions because of their passivity and/or low intellectual capacity. In such cases a *folie à deux* (folly for two) relationship develops. This is a psychiatric disorder in which a more passive and suggestible individual takes on the psychopathology of a more assertive and domineering individual.

During my residency days, the power of the delusion was well illustrated by the anecdote about the interchange between a paranoid psychotic man and a psychiatrist.

Psychiatrist: So what's the problem?
Patient: I'm dead.

Psychiatrist: Are you sure?

Patient: Yes.

Psychiatrist: Well, tell me then, can a dead man bleed?

Patient: No, of course not. Dead people can't bleed.

Psychiatrist (The psychiatrist then takes out a sterile needle, pricks the man's finger, and expresses a drop of blood.): Well, what do you think about that?

Patient: Well, what do you know? This is the first time in the history of the world that a dead man has bled.

The anecdote serves as a good example of the "no win situation" that people face when they try to dispel a delusion by logical thinking. It just does not work. The power of the forces that contribute to the creation of the delusion are so great, and the need to maintain it so strong, that simple logical arguments will not suffice. Most psychiatrists agree that the psychotherapeutic treatment of such patients is most often futile, so powerful is the need to maintain the delusion, so great are the forces operative in its formation and perpetuation.

REACTION FORMATION

Another mechanism operative in such accusations is that of *reaction formation*, in which an individual consciously adopts thoughts, feelings, and behaviors that are opposite to those that are unconsciously harbored. Reaction formation is basically a method for strengthening the projective process. Phenomenologically, it involves repetitious condemnation of the party who is being used as the focus of one's projections. People exhibiting this phenomenon basically say: "If there's one thing I hate in this world it's pedophiles. Accordingly, I will devote myself to their extermination, even if I have to use my last ounce of energy." Proselytizing and campaigns of vilification are embarked upon. The end goal of this ostensibly noble cause is to remove entirely "every God-damn pedophile from the face of the earth." Psychologically, such individuals are ever fighting to repress their own unacceptable pedophilic impulses, which are continually pressing for release. During their harangues against the "perverts" who are the objects of their scorn, they often rise to a level of excitation that can readily be seen as sexual. It should come as no surprise, therefore, when such individuals are found to be exhibiting the very same behavior they have devoted their lives to exterminating. This phenomenon is sometimes referred to as the "return of the repressed."

VOYEURISM

Voyeurism refers to the compulsive need to observe sexual objects or encounters. A "Peeping Tom" is a good example of the voyeur. The opposite of voyeurism is exhibitionism, in which the individual has a strong need to expose oneself or perform sexually in front of others. The voyeur and the exhibitionist need each other. Some individuals are consciously aware of their voyeuristic tendencies and will act out on them with varying degrees of self-acceptance. Others, however, may not be willing to accept their voyeuristic impulses, may suppress and repress them, but will need some kind of release for these desires. Here, I focus on those who have inordinate voyeuristic needs (greater than the normal amount) and who feel guilty over them. Accordingly, they require mechanisms for release that operate unconsciously in the service of assuaging guilt.

There is no question that sexual abuse cases may be "turn ons" for the wide variety of individuals involved in them: the accuser(s), the prosecutors, the lawyers, the judges, the evaluators, the psychologists, the reporters, the readers of the newspapers, and everyone else involved—except for the falsely accused and the innocent victim. And this is one of the great paradoxes of these cases of false accusations. Everyone is getting their "jollies," except the two central figures, who are not only getting little if any sexual pleasure out of the whole thing but whose lives are being destroyed in the process.

RELEASE OF ANGER

Dealing with anger has been one of mankind's central problems. Fight and flight are the animals' primary methods for survival when confronted with danger. Just as fear mobilizes the flight reaction, anger mobilizes the fight reaction. Just as we run faster and more efficiently when we are afraid, we fight harder and more efficiently when we are angry. Anger arises when we are confronted with a noxious stimulus which we wish to remove. The inability to remove quickly the noxious stimulus results first in frustration. And frustration is an uncomfortable emotion that is eliminated by the successful attainment of the goal of removal of a noxious stimulus. When, however, we are unsuccessful in removing the stimulus and frustration mounts, we become angry. The mild state of irritation associated with frustration might not have been successful in serving as a motivating force for the removal of the noxious stimulus. Perhaps in the state of anger the individual will become more efficient and effective in removing the pain.

Because life inevitably produces frustrations, anger is ubiquitous. A central problem for mankind has been to deal effectively with anger. Too much freedom for release of anger would result in a world fraught with danger in which we would live in a constant state of vigilance—ever expecting harm from those around us. Too much suppression and repression of anger results in the damming up of this important emotion and the formation of a wide variety of psychopathological mechanisms that often allow symbolic release. Accordingly, some mid-point has to be found. Actually, human beings and society together have devised a wide variety of mechanisms for anger release. A few examples: Wars sanction murderous rage and even provide honors for those who are most successful in this venture. Sports provide social sanction for the participants to vent competitive hostility on their opponents. Spectators can enjoy vicariously the same phenomenon. Literature, cinema, and television also provide vicarious release. Exercise, political campaigns, and dedication to worthy causes that focus on the removal of deplorable conditions can also serve to release anger. In contrast, too much suppression of anger can contribute to the development of a wide variety of symptoms such as depression, obsessions, compulsions, phobias, paranoia, and persecutory hallucinations.

A wide variety of other mental mechanisms can serve to release anger in socially acceptable ways without the individual's feeling guilt over such release. These mechanisms are especially attractive to those who are inordinately guilty over their angry thoughts and feelings. A sex abuse accusation can serve this purpose quite well. Mention has been made of its value for a wife who wishes to wreak vengeance on her estranged husband. Murder and physically maiming the man may be the only weapons that are more effective than the sex abuse accusation. In the nursery school and day-care center situation, more than one person can be implicated, thus providing a setting for even greater release of pent-up hostility. One alleged perpetrator is then replaced by two, three, four, and even more. Yet we still have only one accuser.

When the accuser joins forces with others, they provide each other with support and justification for anger release, and each one feeds on the other's rage. What may have started off as an individual parent's concern becomes built up into a worthy cause in which all the individuals become obsessed with destroying the alleged perpetrators. Anger tends to feed on itself. When anger builds up into states of rage and fury, its release goes beyond its original purpose(s). One stab in the heart is generally enough to kill an individual; a dozen stabs serve no additional purpose with regard to the original goal. However, the additional 11 thrusts in the chest result from the derangement that anger produces related to the "feeding on itself" phenomenon. And the same mechanism operates in the campaigns against nursery and day-care center personnel accused of sexually abusing children. These innocents have indeed become scapegoats for the pent-up hostilities of the parents, who have now found a socially acceptable and even praiseworthy release for pent-up anger that has its roots in frustrations having absolutely nothing to do with the nursery school. This too is a central element in prejudice: "All of our troubles are caused by those low-life people who live over there. If we eliminate them entirely, all our problems will be solved!"

Recently, I saw a television program on which William Moyers was interviewing William Schirer, the journalist and author. Schirer began his career in Europe during the 1930s and was one of the earliest reporters of the rise to power of the Nazis. Since that time he has written many books on the subject and is generally considered one of the world's foremost authorities on Nazi Germany. Near the end of the program Moyers asked Schirer if he could explain what it was about the German people that enabled them to involve themselves in such atrocities. Much to my surprise Schirer responded that he did not know. In the 50 years during which he had studied the problem, he claimed that he still did not have the faintest idea about what it was about the German people that enabled them to involve themselves in such a holocaust.

I wish I had been on that program. If I were, I would have said: "I have the answer for you. You may not believe this, but it's quite simple. The Germans are no different from the rest of us. We are all capable of such atrocities. All one needs are widespread privation and clever provocateurs and any nation on earth could be brought down to the same levels of debasement. We like to think that we are better than they, those Germans, and that such a thing could not happen in our country (wherever it may be). This is self-deception in the service of exonerating ourselves from the same propensities.

Milgram (1974) demonstrated this principle quite well in a well-known study. He was planning to go to Germany to do a study on the slavish dependence on authority that the Germans appear to have, a dependency that enabled them to commit the aforementioned atrocities with the excuse that they were only "following orders." Before embarking on his study in Germany, he decided to obtain normative baseline data here in the United States on individuals who presumably had no such tendencies. The study involved "ordering" subjects to administer progressively higher doses of electric shock to other "subjects" in order to help them learn better by avoiding the punishment of being shocked when their memory failed. His "normal" Americans exhibited such high levels of authority dependence as well as willingness to administer these shocks that Milgram realized that it was not likely that the Germans would exceed his Americans in this area. Accordingly, Milgram never went to Germany (at least for the purpose of conducting this study).

I recognize that it is not fair to compare the late-twentieth-century sex abuse hysteria in the United States with the Nazi movement in Germany during the 1930s and 1940s. It is not fair only in the terms of the quantity of the destruction of human lives that has resulted. It is fair in terms of the similarity of the mechanisms that were operative. In this section I have focused only on the socially sanctioned release of rage that is apparent in both phenomena. In other places in this book I describe other mechanisms of similarity.

DISPLACEMENT OF BLAME

Sex abuse experts and "validators" (to be discussed below) have provided parents with an excellent opportunity to blame others for the psychological symptoms their children may exhibit—symptoms which have resulted from their own impairments in child rearing. Validators have presented us with an ever-growing list of "indicators," that is, behavioral manifestations that alert parents to the presence of sex abuse. It is of interest that most of these are to be found in the normal repertoire of every child's behavior, for example, nightmares, irritability, bedwetting, behavioral fluctuations, temper tantrums, and masturbation (especially masturbation!). Other such indicators include a wide variety of symptoms that usually have many other causes, for example, conduct disturbances, phobias, depression, and just about any other symptom that one finds in the diagnostic manual of mental disorders. Parents who need to blame others for the presence of these behavioral manifestations (either normal or abnormal, especially abnormal) find an easy scapegoat in the alleged perpetrator. They are essentially saying: "Not only is he (she) responsible for sexually abusing my child, but he (she) has also brought about the wide variety of derivative behavioral disturbances that are causing me and my child such grief." Once again, the guilt-assuaging benefit of the utilization of this maneuver is obvious.

Not all children, of course, begin with any of these behavioral manifestations or indicators. This is especially the case for those who originally state that they were not sexually abused or molested in any way whatsoever. However, as the investigations progress, as the inquiries steam up, these children too develop symptomatic indicators. In part, these are the result of the children's wish to supply the examiners with the answers they wish to receive. Even worse, however, is that many of these symptoms are the *result* of the numerous interrogations to which these children are subjected. Typically, in the course of the evaluations and the subsequent "therapy," there is a progressive "uncovering" process in which more symptoms are both elicited and exhibited. Rather than the examiner considering the possibility that these symptoms are related to the stresses of the interrogations, they conclude that they are "proof" that the abuse has indeed taken place. Human beings are famous for their capacity to fulfill their own prophecies, especially prophecies of despair and doom. Validators can accomplish this quite well via the manipulation of the children in their charge and the parents who gullibly go along with their schemes.

SUBSTITUTION

In situations, especially intrafamilial, in which genuine sex abuse takes place, one mechanism that is often operative is that of *substitution*. For example, a mother who is sexually inhibited may view sexual encounters with loathing. Consciously or unconsciously she facilitates the father's turning his sexual attentions to her daughter in order to "get him off her back" (or "front," as the case may be). In this way, she avoids involving herself in the "disgusting" activities and yet allows "the beast" to gratify his primitive needs and keep him "tamed" and out of "trouble" (being involvement with other women). A common complaint made by women who were sexually abused in childhood is that their mothers did not believe them when they complained about the abuse or refused to talk about it with them. Of course, many factors can be operative in such a mother's rejection. Denial is one of them. To listen to the child with receptivity is to accept the fact that such a heinous crime is being committed in one's own home. Another factor relates to the substitution mechanism. If the mother were to be receptive to the child's complaints, the next obvious step would be to bring about a cessation of the abuse of the child. However, the result of this might be the father's turning to the mother for her involvement in "despicable acts."

The same mechanism may be operative in a sex abuse allegation. Here, the mother is not actually using the child as a substitute for herself, but psychologically gratifying the same desires with the visual imagery that the sex abuse allegation provides. There is overlap here, then, with the vicarious gratification mechanism.

SUGGESTIBILITY AND THE MASS HYSTERIA PHENOMENON

Human beings are extremely suggestible. Even those who claim immunity to such influence are more suggestible than they would like to believe. I consider myself to be an individual who is particularly resistant to such influences, but cannot claim full immunity. I recall well an experience I had in the early 1970s, when extremely wide ties were in vogue. I considered them grotesque and absolutely refused to involve myself in the fad. I knew that it was spawned by the collusion of Madison Avenue (the advertising industry) and Seventh Avenue (the clothing industry) to convince a gullible public that old narrow ties should be discarded and that the new "in" wider (and not incidentally much more expensive) ties were "beautiful." I knew also that after continual exposure to wide ties in the public media and among my friends and colleagues, I would ultimately come to actually believe that my thin ties were indeed "ugly." And, in spite of my complete awareness of the process of indoctrination, I finally did reach the point where I actually looked at my thin ties and really believed that they were ugly. The vignette is presented not simply as an example of human suggestibility but human fear of being considered atypical.

Anyone can be made to believe anything. Hermann Goebbels, Adolph Hitler's propaganda minister, operated on the principle that if one tells people a lie long enough—any lie—the vast majority will come to believe it. But we do not have to go that far back to see the same phenomenon operative in our leaders in recent years. Richard Nixon—ever with a straight face—denied to the end significant involvement in the Watergate imbroglio. Of course, he knew quite well the depth of his involvement and the extent of his duplicity. He also knew quite well that as long as he kept denying involvement, there would always be a significant percentage of the public who would believe him—compelling evidence of guilt notwithstanding. He could rely on millions of people to deny the obvious as long as he staunchly and unswervingly maintained his innocence. Any admission of guilt, however, would weaken significantly—but not destroy entirely (such is the power of the mind to deny)—the fortress of lies that he had created to protect himself. Ronald Reagan utilized the same maneuver in association with the Iran-contra scandal. His basic position was to quizzically say, "I don't know what you're talking about. I've always been a very busy man and I can't be expected to keep on top of everything that goes on in so complex a structure as the United States government." He knew quite well that as long as he maintained this position, millions would deny the evidence for his obvious implication. The late Ferdinand Marcos, the deposed leader of the Philippines, utilized the same maneuvers when confronted with his theft of millions of dollars from his government. His basic response to his accusers: "Swiss bank accounts? I don't know what you're talking about. Property? Houses? Estates? Not mine!"

Our minds are not only malleable with regard to the imposition of others' opinions on us, but we ourselves are powerful self-deceivers in accordance with our own wishes and aspirations. Material that we store in memory does not sit there like rocks in a box, unchanged over years. Rather, our memories become restructured, almost from the moment of "storage." And the nature of the restructuring process is determined by our wishes and aspirations. In fact, there is a censoring and filtration process that selects along the input process and stores only those external stimuli that we want to store, for whatever reason. All of us, if we think about it, can provide examples from our own lives. I have a friend, approximately my own age, whom I've known since childhood (over a span of 50 years). He is an extremely intelligent individual whose brilliance has enabled him to hold a wide variety of extremely important positions in our society. It is not uncommon for us to swap jokes when we get together. The following interchange has occurred on a couple of occasions:

Mike: That joke you just told has always been a favorite of mine, but you know I was the one who first told it to you.

Dick: You know, Mike, I have great respect for you and I believe that you are basically an honest person. I know that you believe you're telling me the truth when you tell me that it was *you* who first told *me* that joke. But you're wrong, it was *I* who first told *you* that joke.

Mike: You know I consider you to be an honest person and I don't believe that you're lying when you tell me that you first told *me* that joke. But I *know* that it was *I* who first told *you* that joke.

Dick: I know, Mike, that you *actually believe* that you told me that joke. No one is free from delusions, but I would be willing to go on the witness stand and swear by everything that's holy to me that it was *I* who first told *you* that joke. (Of course, both of us are now laughing.)

Mike: I really believe that you're telling me the truth when you state that you believe that I'm delusional and that it was you who first told me that joke. But it is you who are delusional here.

Both of us genuinely believe that we are being honest. Obviously, one of us is distorting here. Presumably, we are both very intelligent individuals and we like to consider ourselves to be basically honest in our dealings with one another. I do not really know whether it is Mike or I who has distorted reality here. What I do know is that the interchange is a testament to the capacity of the human mind to distort reality.

Another example: When I was in college, I generally tried to purchase second-hand books because I could ill afford to buy new ones. I recall, at the beginning of my freshman year, purchasing a battered edition of the textbook on contemporary civilization. As I recall, the title was *Introduction to Contemporary Civilization in the West*. I brought it home and embarked on my first reading assignment. With pencil in hand I was prepared to underline what I considered to be the important passages in the assignment. Much to my chagrin I noted that there had been at least *three* previous owners, each of whom had used the underlining technique. I quickly realized that each had used a different color (black, red, and green) in order to ensure that one's underline was truly his (there were no hers at Columbia College in those days). I noted also that there was very little overlap regarding what each of my three predecessors considered to be worthy of underlining. I noted also that what I considered important to underline did not coincide with the selections of any of the three previous owners of the book. I decided then that I would have to use brackets if I were to be able to isolate my own selections from those of the others. (Incidentally, to this day I rarely underline; rather, I use brackets.) I also realized at that point that we differed significantly regarding what we considered important and what we considered unimportant. There was a highly selective process that was determined more by internal psychological processes than by the material on the page. I present this vignette here because it serves as an excellent demonstration of the filtering and censorship process that is internally derived rather than externally imposed.

One last example. As the reader may know, I lecture extensively throughout the United States and occasionally abroad. In the course of each of my lectures, I interrupt and invite questions from the audience. On many occasions a participant will take issue with one of my points, sometimes angrily so. Many times I will respond, "Do you realize that the statement you attributed to me is exactly opposite to what I said. My distinct recollection is that I said X, and not minus X." Sometimes other individuals in the audience will agree with me that the criticizer has completely missed my point and heard exactly the opposite of what I have stated. Embarrassed, somewhat confused, and often incredulous, the party will sit down—often grumbling. At that point I have often said to the group something along these lines:

> What has just happened, I believe, is an excellent example of the way human memory can distort. I believe that if I had made a videotape of the presentation I have just given and then handed out a test of multiple choice, objective questions based on what I have just presented, most if not all of you would miss one or more questions. And each of you would swear by everything that's holy to him or her that I had said something entirely different from what you had just heard. We

would then turn to the videotape and get its "opinion" regarding what I actually said. We would have to agree, then, that you had not processed with 100 percent accuracy my comments and that distortions had crept in. Most often these distortions relate to wishes that I had said the opposite or related to tensions and anxieties engendered by my comments. Furthermore, I am sure that were I in your position, I, too, would distort in accordance with my own wishes, aspirations, and anxieties.

Sometimes the distortion reveals itself in the participants' comment sheet filled out at the end of the conference. Most often the participants enjoy complete anonymity and so are free to write anything they wish, even criticisms they might be ashamed to admit openly in front of an audience. Here, too, I often see statements made about what I allegedly said, statements that are completely at variance and often entirely opposite to what I indeed had stated. I mention this here because it serves as an excellent example of the phenomenon of memory distortion. And here we are dealing with events that only occurred a few minutes prior to the recollection. If we can distort to such a significant degree with regard to material presented only a few minutes previously, we cannot but wonder about the degree of our distortions for material presented years ago.

Suggestibility is one of the factors operative in one's susceptibility to becoming involved in mass hysteria. It enables individuals to suspend disbelief and accept as valid the exhortations of persuasive leaders, especially those whom we make charismatic (charisma is much more in the eye of the beholder than in the body of the person beheld). We select those leaders (when we have the opportunity) who share our aspirations and who we believe have the power to bring about their fulfillment. If the desire for such fulfillment is strong, we may attribute to our leaders powers that go far beyond what actually exists and may even attribute to them magical and supernatural powers. (Becker [1973] considers this factor to be an important element in understanding the evolution of civilization.) When one combines human suggestibility, magical thinking, and the desire for a powerful leader (to compensate for our feelings of impotence), the ground is set for mass hysteria.

Although many consider themselves independent thinkers, the vast majority are easily swept up with the crowd and go along with the latest trends and fads. Sweeping up a group of people—even to fanatic levels—to espouse some cause is not difficult. Political conventions, religious rallies, and death charges on battlefields are examples of this phenomenon. And the frenetic pitch of parents involved in nursery school sex abuse allegations is another example. They rally. They scream and rant. They demonstrate and march. They do their utmost to attract attention in the public media. They proselytize for converts. The term *mass hysteria* is as applicable here as it was in the Salem witch trials (to be discussed in Chapter Fourteen).

GREED

One of the fringe benefits (often for some the primary motivational factor) for jumping on the bandwagon in a day-care center sex abuse scandal is that one can "sue the school." With approximately one lawyer for every 345 people in the US population (1989 figures), there is a sea of hungry lawyers out there, many of whom are very happy to represent these parents. (This figure was obtained by dividing the U.S. Census Bureau's estimate of the U.S. population in December 1989 [approximately 250 million] by the American Bar Association's figures on the number of practicing lawyers in December 1989 [725,574].) In recent years, lawyers' advertising is no longer considered unethical. Accordingly, they are free to "drum up business" wherever and whenever they can. I know of one case in which lawyers literally swooped down on the homes of the children involved in a nursery school scandal and not only offered to represent them on a contingency basis—that is, the clients would pay nothing but the lawyers would receive a share of the settlement (usually one-third to one-half)—but also offered to provide "validators" who would verify that the sex abuse did indeed take place. I cannot imagine, though, that this is an isolated incident and I would suspect that the practice is commonplace.

Traditionally, a claim is made for the payment of the "therapy," which we are led to understand may take many years—even for children who allege only one momentary sexual contact (such as "he once put his hand on my 'gina' over my clothes"). In addition, the parents also ask for punitive damages to compensate the family for the psychological trauma resulting from the sex abuse. When everyone in the day-care center is jumping on the bandwagon, it is hard not to do so as well. And when the rallies are conducted in which a parade of "experts" fires up the crowd to "take action now," all vibrate together and move en bloc to espouse the worthy cause while carrying the banner "believe the children." Of course, personal gain is denied with regard to the million dollars or so frequently asked. Rather, this sum is supposed to help the school to remember not to expose innocent children to such perverts ever again. Considering the fact that in most states there is no "cap" on the amount of money a jury can award to a plaintiff, and considering society's strong and often exaggerated reactions to sex abuse (to be described in Chapter Thirteen), the lawyers and parents can generally expect the jury to be *very* sympathetic to their demands.

In a sense, many of these parents are also victims. They are victims of their gullibility—believing that an "expert"—especially one with an impressive title such as M.D. or Ph.D.—must be providing valid information. They are victims of their dependency on these authorities. And many are victims of their greed, which is so enormous that they blind themselves to the psychological traumas they are subjecting their children to in the service of winning lawsuits that promise them enormous wealth.

6

THE "VALIDATORS" AND OTHER EXAMINERS

I recognize that I am extremely critical of many (and probably most) of the people who are doing evaluations in sex abuse cases. I appreciate that there are some (but I believe they are in the minority) who are conducting skillful evaluations that are balanced and unbiased. My experience, however, has been that the vast majority of those evaluators whose examinations I have had the opportunity to evaluate in depth exhibit significant deficiencies in their techniques. It is this group that I am referring to in this chapter, and it is this group that is playing a significant role in the present sex abuse fiasco. One cannot possibly know the exact percentage of evaluators who fall into the category that I am criticizing here. Furthermore, even that division is artificial in that each evaluator falls at some point along a continuum—from those who manifest most, if not all, of the deficiencies described here to the most competent and skilled who exhibit few, if any, of them. Although their percentage is not certain (and cannot probably be known), there is no question that there are enough of these inadequate and incompetent evaluators to warrant the criticisms presented here.

I suspect that those who refer to themselves as "validators" are most likely performing at the levels of incompetence described in this chapter. The very fact that they are comfortable referring to themselves as validators provides strong justification for my placing them in this category. The name implies that their sole purpose is to *validate* or confirm that the abuse took place. It is the equivalent of a criminal court judge referring to himself as the "convictor" or the "incarcerator." Examiners who read this and find themselves angry and offended might give serious consideration to the possibility that there is validity to my criticisms and that rectification of the problem might be warranted. Those who respond to such irritation by not giving any consideration to the possibility that my criticisms are valid are likely to be depriving themselves of the opportunity to learn some useful principles and interviewing techniques.

WHO ARE THESE PEOPLE?

There is no generally recognized training program for sex abuse evaluators. The field is basically "open territory." Some have training in psychology, some in social work, and many in various aspects of "social service." Many are self-styled "therapists" who have absolutely no training at all, even in related disciplines. It is important for the reader to appreciate that all states have specific requirements for certification in such disciplines as psychiatry, clinical psychology, and clinical social work. States vary, however, regarding their receptivity to providing certification for family counselors, pastoral counselors, nurse practitioners, and other types of mental health professionals. I do not know of a state (and there may be one or more) that provides certification for therapists. In most states (to the best of my knowledge), anyone can hang up a shingle and say that he (she) is a therapist, and one cannot be prevented from practicing because of the failure to have certification or a license. In short, one cannot be penalized for practicing without a license if one does not have to have a license in the first place.

Some of these self-styled therapists have also crept into the sex abuse field, where they serve as not only evaluators but therapists as well. Sex abuse is a "growth industry." Until recently, they tell us, when we were not aware of how widespread the sex abuse phenomenon was, we did not train many individuals who were qualified to conduct such evaluations and provide appropriate treatment. Now we have come to appreciate how limited are the number of people available to take on the monumental task of processing all these cases. Legislators are bombarded with requests to provide more money to train and recruit such personnel. Because of the great demand for their services and the paucity of highly qualified people, standards are lowered, requirements are ill-defined, and a wide variety of obvious incompetents are conducting such evaluations and treatment.

Many of these ill-qualified and incompetent people take "courses" in which they are trained by others of questionable qualifications. What happens then is that the misinformation, ignorance, and gullibility of the teachers gets passed on to their students and so on down the generations. Unfortunately, most students (happily not all) take a very passive and receptive view of their instructors. They make the assumption that the teachers must know what they are talking about or otherwise they wouldn't be in their position of authority. Walk into any classroom (even in the most prestigious colleges) and one will see an army of students, writing down reflexly what their instructors are saying. The "best" students are those who regurgitate what they have been asked to memorize. Even in the best schools this process takes place. I believe that only a very small percentage of students are actually encouraged to question the authority of their instructors and to genuinely think independently and creatively. It is no surprise then that evaluators, who have most often had limited and even inferior educational experiences, are even more prone to accept as gospel what they are taught in these courses. Even I, who have provided expert testimony in courts on this subject, *never* received formal training (during my medical school, internship, and residency days in the 1950s) for differentiating between bona fide and fabricated sex abuse allegations. However, I have at least had many years of training in related fields—psychiatry, psychology, child development, and medicine—which have served as a foundation for my subsequent three decades of experience in this realm.

Most sex abuse workers operate in the context of a government agency, referred to in many states as the Child Protection

Team (CPT) or Child Protection Service (CPS). Many unashamedly refer to themselves as "validators." Those who utilize this term make no secret of the fact that the vast majority (if not all) of the children they have evaluated have been sexually abused. As implied in their name, they are merely there to "validate" what everybody knows happened anyway. Otherwise, why would the child be brought forth? I am certain that a judge who referred to himself (herself) as a "convictor" would not be considered to have the neutrality that we expect of people in such positions. Yet, we say little about validators and the obvious bias implied in their very title. In their partial (I emphasize the word partial here) defense, many of these people have been working in settings where the vast majority of referrals relate to intrafamilial sex abuse, where the prevalence of genuine abuse is quite high. They have had little experience in vicious child custody disputes and day-care center allegations, where the incidence is quite low. They have had little experience with making the differentiations necessary when evaluating referrals in the latter categories. Accordingly, they tend to assume that what was valid in the intrafamilial situation is valid in other situations as well. This could have been a rectifiable problem. Unfortunately, for the reasons provided throughout this book, this problem was not addressed adequately or soon enough, thereby contributing to the prevention of the mass hysteria phenomenon that we are experiencing at this time.

WHAT DO THEY DO?

To date, I have spent about 150 hours viewing and analyzing the videotapes of these examiners, and I have about 1,500 hours (my best estimate) reviewing their reports and reading their depositions and testimonies. Although such materials have been sent to me from various parts of the United States, it is amazing how similar the techniques are. Accordingly, I consider myself to be in a good position to describe in detail exactly what these examiners do. In fact, because they work so similarly—regardless of what part of the country they operate in—it is easy to make some generalizations about their techniques.

"Children Never Lie"

In order to justify and advance their prediction that the child will be found to be abused, they espouse the dictum that "children never lie" on all issues related to sex abuse. The reasoning goes that a young child, having had absolutely no exposure to or experience with sexual encounters, must be telling the truth if such an encounter is described. A related slogan is "believe the children." Even those who have had children themselves, and deal daily with the fabrications and delusions of their own children, have no problem waving these banners. In order to maintain this position they must deny the "polymorphous perversity" that Freud described almost a hundred years ago and that all parents (if they will only just look and listen) have to accept as a reality of childhood. They have to believe that the sex abuse prevention programs to which many of their evaluees have already been exposed are in no way a contaminant to their investigatory process. They have to believe, as well, that there has been no coaching or programming (overt or covert, conscious or unconscious) by the parents who bring their children to them, even though a vicious child custody dispute may be taking place or the child is one of many parading out of a nursery school in which there is an atmosphere of mass hysteria. They have to deny, as well, the previously described ubiquity of sexual stimuli in our society.

Ascertaining Whether the Child Can Differentiate Between the Truth and a Lie

Early in the interview these examiners first satisfy themselves that the child can differentiate between the truth and the lie. In many states, the judge, lawyers, and all other investigators are required by statute to submit to this requirement before proceeding with the substantive issues in the interview. For example, when examining children in the three-to-five-year age level, a typical maneuver in the service of satisfying this requirement is for the examiner to point to a red object and say to the child, "This is *red*. Is that the truth or a lie?" If the child answers that the examiner is being truthful

("That's true"), the examiner may then proceed by pointing to something that is green and saying, "This is black. Is that the truth or a lie?" If the child then states that the examiner is then "lying," the examiner may then proceed to a series of other equally asinine questions in order to demonstrate that the child knows the difference between the truth and a lie.

The same child is not asked the question, "Santa Claus brings you gifts at Christmas time. Is that the truth or a lie?" "The good fairy left money under your pillow after your tooth fell out. Is that the truth or a lie?" Obviously, asking any question that would be more complex—one that might result in the child's demonstrating confusion between fact and fantasy—would confront the examiner with the obvious fact that young children have great difficulty differentiating between fact and fantasies, between the truth and a lie, in a wide variety of areas. As mentioned previously, we adults are not famous for our capacity to make such differentiations either. Ignoring this obvious fact enables such examiners to proceed with the "validation." Nor do they set up situations in which the child is likely to lie, such as when accused of a transgression. Children traditionally lie under such circumstances, but to demonstrate this in the interview would, of course, raise questions about the child's veracity regarding the sexual abuse issue.

What is also ignored is the fact that *knowing the difference* between the truth and a lie is very different from the issue of whether or not the child *will actually* lie. These evaluators make the very naive assumption that because the child knows the difference between the truth and a lie, that the child will not lie. The vast majority of people who commit crimes know quite well the difference between the truth and a lie; yet, they still lie, especially in response to questions that might divulge their guilt. The whole inquiry regarding differentiating between the truth and a lie is a mockery, a sham, a ritual that these people go through in order to convince themselves that they are indeed getting to "the truth."

Naming the Body Parts

The next step in a typical evaluation is to bring out some pictures of naked people, the ostensible purpose of which is to find out what names the particular child being interviewed uses for the various organs and orifices that are to be found on the human body. I have not yet seen or heard of an examiner who will ask the mother questions regarding what terms the child uses for these body parts. To do so would deprive the examiner of the opportunity to introduce the subject of sexuality at the outset, which is what the discussion of naming body parts is really all about. Typically, these examiners are oblivious to the importance of the psychological blank screen (like the blank card on the *Thematic Apperception Test [TAT]* [Murray, 1936]) as the most valid way of obtaining information about what's going on in a person's mind. (The TAT is a psychological test in which the patient is presented with a series of cards, each of which depicts a somewhat vague scene, and the patient is asked to describe what is going on. There is no "right" answer and the projections so elicited provide the examiner with information about the psychological processes that are operative in the patient's mind. The blank card, in which there are no external stimuli, is the most anxiety-provoking—but at the same time the most revealing—of the series of cards.) Sometimes the so-called "anatomically correct dolls" (see below) are brought out at this point to serve the same purpose, namely, to ascertain the names the child uses for the various sexual organs.

These examiners do not seem to appreciate that the anatomical pictures and dolls are different from just about anything the child has previously seen and are likely to produce strong emotional reactions. This serves to obfuscate and suppress other emotions (having nothing to do with sex abuse) that may be at the forefront of the child's mind. Also, they transmit to the child the message that the examiner is interested in discussing matters related to naked bodies and this serves to draw the child's thoughts, fantasies, and feelings into that path. Whether the examiner uses the pictures or the dolls, a significant contamination has been introduced at the outset, a contamination that already makes it unlikely that the examiner will truly find out whether the child has been genuinely abused. After exposure to these pictures or dolls, one cannot know whether the child's verbalizations about sex abuse were the result of an actual experience or were stimulated by the naked human figures.

The So-called
Anatomically Correct Dolls

Anatomically correct dolls (for the reader who does not know about these monstrosities) are dolls that specifically depict genital parts (including pubic hair) and breasts (most often with prominent nipples). Many have gaping orifices (vagina, anus, and mouth). Many cannot be justifiably called "anatomically correct" because of the disproportion between the size of the genitals and the rest of the body. More recently, in order to protect themselves from this criticism, many of these workers have referred to the dolls as "anatomically detailed dolls." No matter what they are called, they are a serious contamination to any meaningful psychiatric interview. Unless the child has been previously evaluated by one of these "validators," it is most likely that the child has never seen such a doll before. The child cannot but be startled and amazed by such a doll. The likelihood of the child's ignoring these unusual genital features is almost at the zero level. Accordingly, the dolls almost demand attention and predictably will bring about the child's talking about sexual issues. Again, the contamination here is so great that the likelihood of differentiating between bona fide and fabricated sex abuse has become reduced considerably by the utilization of these terrible contaminants.

If one gives a child a peg and a hole, the child is going to put the peg in the hole unless the child is retarded or psychotic. Give a child a wooden doughnut; the child will inevitably place his (her) fingers in the hole. Give a child one of these female anatomical dolls with wide open mouth, anus, and vagina; the child will inevitably place one or more fingers in one of these conspicuous orifices. For many of these workers, such an act is "proof" that the child has indeed been sexually abused. The assumption is made that what the child does with these dolls is an exact, point-by-point replication of what has occurred in reality. The argument goes that these dolls "help" the child verbalize what has happened. Presumably, they help the child overcome cognitive and verbal immaturities or psychological tensions and anxieties that interfere with direct discussion of the abuse. And this is a basic premise upon which these people work. All this is crass rationalization. It justifies the use of these materials to verify what the examiner believes in the first place, namely, that the sex abuse did occur. No competent psychologist or psychiatrist believes that the child's projections on the Rorschach, Thematic Apperception Test, or doll play necessarily reflect reality. What they do reflect is the child's cognitive processes, wishes, aspirations, and distortions—although they certainly could include reality elements.

These examiners do not consider the obvious alternative that what the child does with these dolls may have nothing at all to do with what has taken place in reality. But, of course, if they consider this possibility, then they have greater difficulty "proving" the sex abuse, which is what they are there to validate. With such a premise, it is no surprise that many of these examiners claim to have seen hundreds of children in succession, all of whom have demonstrated that they have been sexually abused. In the course of playing with these dolls, it is almost inevitable that the child will take the penis (often erect) and place it in one of the orifices of the female doll. And this, of course, "proves" that the child engaged in the activity depicted by the insertion, namely, fellatio, vaginal intercourse, or anal intercourse.

Even if the child is two years old and even if the insertion of the alleged perpetrator's penis into the child's vagina would produce lacerations, abrasions, contusions, severe bleeding, and pain (inevitably the case when an attempt is made to place an adult male penis into a two-year-old's vagina), the examiner concludes that the sexual intercourse did take place because it was demonstrated during doll play. What is one of the great paradoxes of this field is that some of these examiners are indeed trained clinical psychologists (some even have Ph.D. degrees) and utilize projective instruments as a vehicle for learning about the child's fantasies, wishes, aspirations, and distortions. Yet, in the same report, when the child projects material about sex abuse onto these dolls, the assumption is made that here the child is telling the truth. This cognitive "splitting" on the part of such examiners is testament to the power of the human mind to deceive itself in the service of one's wishes, in this case the wish to see sex abuse.

Sophisticated and sensitive clinicians allow a child to begin a session by scanning and selecting from an array of materials that are available for play evaluation and therapy. They recognize that the child's selection will be determined by the psychological processes that are pressing for expression. They appreciate that the toy so selected will be the one that is most likely to serve as a catalyst for the expression of those thoughts and feelings that are most important for the child to reveal at that moment. Validators have little if any appreciation of this phenomenon. Many of these examiners often have nothing else on their shelves but the anatomical dolls and, even if they do, do not allow the child free play and selection. Rather, validators confront the child with the dolls immediately. Of course, there are some examiners who do indeed allow the free play. However, the actual presence of such dolls is such a significant contaminant that I would consider any examiner who utilizes them to be incompetent. I am not alone in this regard. In the state of California, testimony based on information elicited from such dolls may not be admissible in court. It is my hope that other states will soon follow suit.

Leading Questions

Most of these examiners seem to be oblivious to the value of the open-ended question, the question that has a universe of possible responses. It is not pure chance that competent examiners begin each session with questions such as "So what's on your mind?" and "What would you like to talk about today?" The equivalent opening for young children is to allow the child free play in the playroom in order to choose whatever object is desired. Well-trained examiners appreciate that the best toys for projection are those that have the fewest contaminating stimuli. Accordingly, play objects such as blocks, sand, clay, crayons, and blank paper serve well in this regard because they do not have any intrinsic contaminations to the pure projections. Dolls are less valuable for this purpose but, because they resemble human beings, are more likely to catalyze projections related to human relationships. However, experienced examiners recognize that the fewer details the doll has, the better it will serve as a stimulus for the child's uncontaminated projections.

Validators do not seem to appreciate these well-established principles of child psychological evaluation and treatment. Well-trained examiners recognize also that all play equipment are props and should only be used when the examiner cannot elicit the desired material by using verbal catalysts. They know also that the best verbal catalysts are questions of the aforementioned type, which do not include any specific references to any particular issue. Rather, the questions are designed to facilitate the expression of a universe of possible thoughts and feelings. What the child selects from that universe is therefore highly meaningful and provides the examiner with useful information about what is going on in the child's mind. Even a request like "Tell me about school" is not a good one to begin with because it directs the child to only one of the universe of possible areas that might have been focused upon.

Validators appear to be oblivious to these important techniques in child evaluation and treatment. Many "zero right in" with their leading questions. Almost invariably, these direct the child to talk about sex abuse. Some typical examples: A three-year-old girl has placed her finger in the vagina of the anatomically correct doll. As mentioned, validators almost invariably consider this to be "proof" that some adult perpetrator has placed his (less often her) finger in the child's vagina. The examiner, without any previous discussion about the child's father, says, "Does your daddy put his fingers in you just like that?" The child may not have been sexually abused and may never even have thought about her father doing such a thing. Yet, the question plants a seed in the child's mind that such an event could possibly take place. Another example: While holding up the chart of a naked woman (allegedly to find out what names the child uses for the various body parts), the examiner asks, "Has your teacher ever touched you there?" The child may never have been abused by her teacher or anyone else. The question introduces the visual image of such an encounter and contaminates, thereby, all further inquiry regarding sex abuse, by the teacher or anyone else for that matter. After that, whether the answer is yes or no (see below), one does not really know whether such an event actually occurred.

Belief in the Preposterous

No matter how preposterous the allegation, no matter how absurd, these examiners will believe them. They have no trouble believing that adult males can have sexual intercourse with two-year-old girls with no evidence of pain, bleeding, and trauma. The facts that the adult male penis cannot be accommodated by the vagina of a two-year-old and that insertion will result in the aforementioned consequences are ignored. They would believe that a child can be forced to drink urine and eat feces and yet, minutes later, be perfectly happy and friendly—without any sign or symptom of the indignities suffered only a few minutes earlier. They would believe that one person was able to undress 25 children, engage them simultaneously in a wide variety of sexual activities, and then dress them quickly in order to be picked up by their parents. And yet, not a single child left wearing the wrong sock, underwear, or other article of clothing. They believe that children can have swords inserted up their rectums with no medical evidence. They believe that children can be smeared with feces and yet be so quickly and thoroughly cleaned that not a scintilla of evidence remains to serve as a clue as to what transpired only a few minutes earlier.

They believe that children can witness the barbecuing of babies, the slaughtering of infants and animals, and their burial in cemeteries, without breathing a word of these activities for weeks and even months after exposure to these atrocities. They can believe that dozens of children can be sworn to silence without ever breathing a word to their parents about any of the tortures to which they have been subjected. They believe that children can be stabbed with scissors, knives, and other instruments in their mouths, ears, noses, vaginas, and anuses, and yet not reveal any signs of their trauma (even on medical examination) only minutes after the event. They believe that bands of men wearing masks and costumes (clowns, big bad wolf costumes, cops, firemen) can enter a school, involve the children in a wide variety of the aforementioned rituals and abuses, and then sneak out, completely unobserved by teachers, parents, and school administrators.

They believe that pedophiles are exceedingly clever and cunning in their methods, so much so that even the most experienced detectives and investigators may find no clues or remnants whatsoever of the wide variety of tortures, rituals, and abuses to which these children have been subjected. Even though no one has ever found any of the dead bodies that these children describe having been buried as a part of their abuse rituals, and even though many cemeteries have been dug up in the search for such bodies, they still believe that such sacrifices indeed took place. Many believe that hundreds of babies have been burned, stabbed, cooked, barbecued, and drowned in the service of warning children that this will happen to them if they breathe a word of their experiences to their parents. Even though not one remnant of any of the aforementioned infants has been found, the belief is still strong. It is as if the "common sense" cells and tracks of their brains have been extirpated by a special operation.

Selective Ignoring of the Impossible

The aforementioned activities, although outlandish and preposterous, are still within the realm of possibility (often narrowly so). When examiners are confronted with information that even they recognize as impossible, then other psychological mechanisms must be utilized in order to maintain the delusion that the child has been sexually abused. For example, in the course of describing the abuse, the child says that her mother (the one who brought about the allegation in the first place) was present at the time when the nursery school teacher fed her "doo-doo." Because the examiner does not believe that this was the case, this bit of information will be disregarded with the excuse that "the child was tired at the time." When the child states that the abuse took place in the examiner's office, a common explanation is "That's her way of saying that she views my office as a 'safe haven' and that's why she spoke about the abuse taking place here." When confronted with inconsistencies that are mutually contradictory and would suggest that one of the versions has to be impossible, the examiner might state: "It's not my job to confront the child with inconsistencies."

Another way of dealing with the introduction of impossible elements into the scenario is to utilize the mechanism of splitting. Specifically, if the child states, for example, that all four grandparents were there and observed the molestation, the examiner might state: "She's confusing two events, the molestation and the family gathering." In this way the sex abuse scenario remains "pure" and its contaminants removed.

Sometimes the examiner does not even feel the need to provide a rationalization for ignoring material that might suggest that the story is not valid. One child claimed that her nursery school teacher had picked up a car and had thrown it into a tree. The examiner unashamedly just stated that, of course, this could not have happened and then went on to accept as valid all other information that supported the conclusion that sex abuse did indeed occur. This selective inattention to noncorroborating data is one of the hallmarks of these validators' interview techniques.

Another maneuver utilized by these examiners is this: "Her denial proves it's true. That's typical of these children who are sexually abused. They keep denying that it happened. That's because they were threatened with terrible consequences if they were to admit it. I've seen many such cases." Another explanation that is provided when a child denies that anything has happened: "She's repressing it. It's been so traumatic to her that she can't talk about it. It may take months of therapy before she'll be able to admit it, even to herself. That's how powerful these repressive forces are." Obviously, there is no way to win for accused people when the child is interviewed by such validators.

The Utilization of the Yes/No Question

Competent examiners recognize the risks of the yes/no question and generally avoid it. They realize that little information is obtained from such a question. (This is something that attorneys and judges have yet to discover.) When one gets a yes or no answer, one does not know whether the interviewee is lying, is telling the truth, or is merely providing an answer (yes or no selected at random) to "get the examiner off his (her) back." Spontaneously verbalized sentences and paragraphs are far better sources of information. These essay-type answers are more likely to be revealing of the child's true thoughts and feelings. But these examiners do not appreciate this obvious fact. Generally, they persist in the inquiry until they get the yeses they want. Often the questions are quite confusing to the child, to the point where the child does not even understand what is being asked. In such an altered state of consciousness, the child is likely to say yes to every question in order to get the examiner to come to the end of the unrelentless series of questions. Because children are suggestible and wish to ingratiate themselves to authority, they may provide all the yes answers the examiner wishes (I will discuss children's suggestibility in greater detail in Chapter Seven.)

The yes/no question is also used in association with the seed-planting phenomenon. On day one the examiner asks the child if she ever had a particular sexual experience—for example, whether her father put his penis in her mouth. (This is a very dangerous thing for an adult male to do to an unreceptive child [unless the child has no teeth].) The child may never have entertained such a fantasy. However, the very question has now planted the seed, and the visual image of such an encounter has now been created in the child's mind. At that point, the child who has never had such an experience will say no. During a subsequent interview, the interviewer (or another examiner) may ask the same question. This time the visual image will be brought out of memory storage and the child may be somewhat confused regarding whether or not such a thing actually happened. A young child may not be able to differentiate between an image that depicts something that actually happened and an image that depicts something that was suggested. In fact, we adults are not immune from such a process either. (Professional brainwashers and propagandists know well that if you tell someone a lie frequently enough, the person will believe it.) If the child then shows some confusion regarding whether such an event actually took place, the examiner is sure to hammer away at the question: "Are you sure?" "Are you sure he didn't do it?" Finally, the child says yes, and that will serve as another nail in the coffin of the accused. This is not only tragic for the falsely accused person, but it is also tragic for the child who is likely to believe for the rest of her (his) life that the event took place.

The So-called Indicators of Sex Abuse

Validators utilize an ever-growing list of "indicators" of sex abuse. These are the behavioral manifestations, which can be observed by parents, that result from sex abuse. These manifestations can be roughly divided into two categories (although there is some overlap). The first is those behaviors that most competent and knowledgeable observers would consider normal. In fact, healthy and knowledgeable parents would also consider these behaviors to be part of the normal child's repertoire. It takes a zealous validator and a gullible parent to share in the delusion that these behavioral patterns are indeed the result of sex abuse. The second category is psychological symptoms, which are listed in the manual of psychiatric disorders. Most competent evaluators recognize that these disorders have a wide variety of causes, most of which have absolutely nothing to do with sex abuse. The validators would consider most of them to result from sex abuse. Of course, this division into two categories is my own; validators have just one long list of behavioral manifestations, all of which derive from sex abuse. I will now provide a few examples from each of these two categories.

"Indicators" That Would Be Considered Normal by Competent Evaluators   Examiners who consider the behavioral manifestations in this category as signs of sex abuse must be abysmally ignorant of normal childhood development. Or, if they have received such training, they have to obliterate from memory what they have learned. Furthermore, if they themselves have children, they must deny their own observations (past or present) regarding the presence of these behaviors in their offspring. The frequency with which they are capable of ignoring what they observe is a testament to the power of the human mind to utilize selective inattention, denial, and projection. Some examples: One doesn't have to be a full professor of pediatrics to know that many children are still bedwetting at ages three and four. This does not prevent validators from considering bedwetting at that age to be a sign of sex abuse.

One does not have to be a full professor of child psychiatry to know that normal children exhibit occasional nightmares, especially in early to mid-childhood. Some of these nightmares are the direct result of frightening experiences such as watching a "scary" movie on television or actually having a frightening experience. Such nightmares are part of the desensitization process that helps children adapt to these frightening exposures. Other nightmares arise sui generis and have complex psychological meanings that are still not completely understood (Gardner, 1986a, 1988b). Validators will typically consider nightmares to be one of the important indicators of sex abuse. Although frequent nightmares of certain types might very well be an indicator of sex abuse, these evaluators typically do not attempt to make any differentiation between normal nightmares and those that might be exhibited by sexually abused children. I have never seen a report in which an inquiry has been made into the frequency of nightmares and their relationship between the described nightmares and the alleged abuse. This is not the way the human mind works. If a nightmare is being used for the purposes of desensitization to a trauma (whether it be sex abuse or another kind of trauma), it is likely to serve this function soon after the abuse—even the first night following the abuse—not months or years later. Validators will ignore this obvious fact in order to justify the use of the nightmare as an indicator of sex abuse.

Furthermore, if the nightmare is to be used as an indicator, one would think that the examiner might want to consider the *content*, especially with regard to the likelihood that it relates to sex abuse. Most validators do not seem to have any need to do this. Any nightmare, regardless of content, is used as an indicator. They can justify this with the old psychoanalytic standby that it represents a symbol for the sex abuse. The most common normal nightmare involves some malevolent entity (a point, a shadow, a monster, a bad man, a bogeyman, etc.) coming menacingly toward the child. Typically, the child wakes up just before the malevolent figure reaches the child. Invariably, evaluators consider this malevolent entity to be symbolic of the alleged sex abuse perpetrator. Whatever the meaning of this nightmare (and my own opinion on its meaning is irrelevant at this point), they do not see the need to explain how the vast majority of nonsexually abused children will have the *same* nightmare. (The reader who is interested in my opinion of the meaning of this common nightmare might wish to refer to my publications on the meaning of children's dreams [1986a, 1988b].) In one case I was involved in, a three-year-old child described how the "big bad wolf" was chasing her in a dream. Predictably, the validator concluded that this dream was proof that the child had

been sexually abused. This child was one of many involved in a
day-care center sex abuse "scandal." The parents actively communicated with one another regarding their children's symptoms and,
not surprisingly, within a few weeks most of the other children were
also reporting big bad wolf nightmares. Rather than consider this to
be the result of the mass hysteria phenomenon, all the validators
concluded that the big bad wolf represented the alleged perpetrator,
an adolescent boy whom I considered to be completely innocent.

The parents are alerted to be on the lookout for any behavioral
changes. Predictably, these are considered to be manifestations of
sex abuse. In order to utilize this criterion, one must ignore the
obvious fact that every child in the history of the world exhibits
behavioral changes, often on a day-to-day basis. Normal children
exhibit behavioral changes; if they did not, they would not be
moving along the developmental track. The one-year-old behaves
differently from the newborn infant; the two-year-old differently
from the one-year-old; the three-year-old differently from the
two-year-old, and so on. Development does not run an even
course; rather, it moves in spurts and plateaus. Furthermore,
children go ahead three steps and go back two steps, and so it goes.
Children have good days and bad days (just like adults). Some of the
behavioral changes that validators will consider manifestations of sex
abuse are an increase in sibling rivalry, refusal to go to sleep,
changing attitudes regarding foods, periods of uncooperative behavior, defiance, and exaggerated reactions to normal disciplinary
measures. In one well-publicized case, the parents informed the
validator that the child had developed an aversion to tuna fish. The
validator quickly concluded that this was yet another proof that the
child had been sexually molested. Her reasoning: The human
vagina, as everyone knows, smells like fish. This child's aversion to
tuna fish must relate to the fact that she had performed cunnilingus
on her nursery school teacher, the alleged perpetrator. With the
utilization of logic like this, it is easy to see how impotent accused
individuals feel when the alleged victims are being evaluated by such
sick and/or ignorant examiners.

The list of indicators that are derived from normal childhood
behavior is long, and there are many other examples. Temper
tantrums are normal, especially between the ages of two and four.

In fact, it is reasonable to say that all children, at some time or another, exhibit temper tantrums. It is the normal, natural, primitive way that children express their anger. Predictably, validators consider temper tantrums to be a manifestation of sex abuse, the child allegedly acting out the anger that was built up against the perpetrator. All siblings exhibit frequent rivalry. In fact, it is ubiquitous. The first-born is generally king (queen) of the world. The second-born now requires that the throne be shared, and worse, the time that the parents must devote to the second is greater than that which must be devoted to the first. This produces even greater rivalrous feelings. And when other children come along, there is even greater resentment over the fact that the parental involvement must be shared among all the children. I would go further and say that children who do not exhibit rivalrous feelings toward their siblings have some form of psychopathology, especially in the area of suppression and repression of their thoughts and feelings. Once again, validators ignore this reality and would consider sibling rivalry to be one of the indicators.

And now to masturbation. All normal children explore their bodies from time to time and do not differentiate between the genital area and other parts. They have to learn from others that touching oneself in that particular area is socially unacceptable, especially in public. Children usually learn by themselves that stimulation of that area can provide pleasures different from those derived from touching other areas. Although orgastic capacity is possible at birth, most young children under the age of nine or ten do not stimulate themselves to the point where they reach orgasm. Those who do may very well have been prematurely introduced into the pubertal and postpubertal levels of sexual arousal. Certainly, such introduction can be the result of sex abuse. But this is not the *only* reason why a younger child might masturbate to orgasm. In some children it is a tension-relieving device, especially when they grow up in homes in which there has been significant privation and/or stress. In some it can serve as an antidepressant. When a knowledgeable evaluator hears that a child is masturbating, the examiner will make detailed inquiry about the frequency, the time of onset, the circumstances under which it occurs, and whether or not the child masturbates to orgasm. All this information is useful in ascertaining whether or not the masturbation is related to sex abuse. Typically, validators do not make such inquiries. They hear the word masturbation and that is enough to prove that the child has been sexually molested.

It is of interest that in the late nineteenth century, in both the United States and England, we witnessed a period of excessive preoccupation and Draconian condemnation of childhood masturbation. Unfortunately, physicians (who should have known better) were actively involved in this campaign of denunciation and attempts to obliterate entirely this nefarious practice. Doctors considered it to be the cause of a wide variety of illnesses, e.g., blindness, insanity, and muscle spasms. Various kinds of restraints were devised in order to prevent children from engaging in this dangerous practice. Some girls were even subjected to clitorectomies, so dangerous was the practice considered to be. Parents were given a long list of symptoms which were considered to be concomitants of masturbation. Some of the alerting signs: temper tantrums, bedwetting, sleep disturbances, appetite changes, mood fluctuations, and withdrawal. Obviously, in the hundred years since those sad times, we seem to have gone back full circle. The same list of symptoms that were indicators of masturbation are now considered to be indicators of sex abuse. Legrand et al. (1989) have written a fascinating article describing the similarities between the masturbation hysteria of the late nineteenth century and the sex abuse hysteria of the late twentieth century, with a comparison of the lists of "indicators."

It is of interest that physicians have played an important role in these crazes. As I will discuss in detail in Chapter Fourteen, it was a doctor (Dr. William Griggs of Salem) who first "diagnosed" the children in the Salem witchcraft trials as being possessed by the devil. Doctors were actively involved in the antimasturbation fanaticism of the late nineteenth century. And, unfortunately, there are "doctors" actively involved in the present fiasco. There are physicians who are diagnosing sex abuse in the vast majority of children they examine, utilizing criteria that are generally considered to be within the normal range (e.g., anal "winking" and hymenal tags). And there are other kinds of doctors (Ph.D. psychologists and M.D. psychiatrists) who are serving as validators and therapists and are perpetrating the abominations described throughout this book.

"Indicators" That Would Be Considered by Competent Observers to Be Symptomatic of Disorders Having Nothing to Do with Sex Abuse.   Here I refer to those symptoms that are to be found in the *Diagnostic and Statistical Manual of the American Psychiatric Association (DSM-III-R)*. If we are to believe the validators, just about any symptom in this manual that could possibly have a psychogenic (or environmental) cause can be a manifestation of sex abuse. These would include depression, phobias, tics, obsessive-compulsive rituals, conduct disorders, antisocial behavior, hyperactivity, attention-deficit disorder, headaches, gastrointestinal complaints (nausea, cramps, diarrhea), musculoskeletal complaints, etc. In short, if there is any possibility of attributing symptoms to sex abuse, the evaluator will do so. It is easier to do this when one is ignorant of the multiplicity of factors that can indeed bring about such disorders. Many validators lack this training and so have no problem with this oversimplified approach to the explanation for these symptoms.

The maneuver utilized here is to assume, often reflexly, that a psychopathological manifestation is the result of sex abuse. In order to do this, the evaluator must make the assumption that the child came from a normal, healthy home and all went well prior to the alleged sex abuse. Typically, these examiners do little if any inquiry into the home situation. Detailed interviews of the parents are quite uncommon; rather, from the outset, the primary (and often exclusive) focus is on the child. Most often the conclusion that the child was sexually abused is made within a few minutes, with absolutely no inquiry into the family background, especially with regard to the presence of factors that might be contributory to the development of psychopathology. Many of the validators would not know how to conduct such an evaluation, so limited has been their training. Obviously, if they were to conduct such inquiries, they might learn that the origin of the symptoms has nothing to do with sex abuse, but is more likely to be the result of psychopathology engendering environmental influences.

Another common maneuver is to attribute to sex abuse the

symptoms that arose directly from the series of interrogations conducted by the validators, lawyers, psychologists, psychiatrists, prosecutors, etc. A detailed history (which most of these individuals fail to take) would quickly indicate that the child's symptoms began at around the time of the interrogations, rather than at the time of the alleged sex abuse. Of course, validators would not want to believe for one moment that their allegedly sensitive and nonintrusive investigations could bring about psychopathology. I consider my own interviews to be sophisticated and to be ones in which I avoid the numerous interview pitfalls and errors described in this book. However, I openly admit that even my interviews may be stressful to children and might contribute to the development of psychopathology. However, in my defense, they are limited to a few interviews and I do not conduct "therapy" for sex abuse, unless I am 100 percent convinced that the abuse has indeed taken place. With regard to the stresses related to the few interviews I do conduct during evaluations, I believe that their effects are small as far as their contribution to producing long-term and even permanent psychopathology. Such stresses are a small price to pay when one considers the terrible consequences to a falsely accused person if the court (and often the jury) is not convinced that the allegation is false. We have to weigh here the trauma to the child caused by my inquiry against the psychological trauma suffered by a falsely accused person—whose life may be destroyed and who may even be incarcerated for many years.

More Direct Coercive Techniques

Although all the aforementioned techniques are, in a sense, coercive, there are some maneuvers that these people utilize that are more obviously so. One is: "I know it happened and I'm going to keep you here until you tell me the truth." Other examples: "Things like this happen to lots of kids. I know many children to whom the same thing happened. Don't worry, I'll protect you." "You can tell me. I'll make sure that he'll never do *that* again." "Now, Bobby, Jamie, Bill, Bob, etc., all told me that it happened to them. Are you going to be the only child in the whole school who is not going to tell me what happened?" "I don't believe that's the only place he touched you. I want you to tell me about the *other* places. You know there *were* other places." The physical torturing of a witness or an accused party is an ancient tradition. Inflict pain on an individual and you are likely to get a confession. These techniques are the modern-day equivalent of physical torture and, like their ancient antecedents, they also work with a high degree of predictability. Our founding fathers presumably ensured (in our Constitution) protection from such tactics for all Americans. Unfortunately, there appear to be some "loopholes" in that these torture techniques are still being utilized.

Involvement with Parents, The Accused, and the Accuser

Typically, these evaluators see little or no need to interview the accused. In fact, I have come across some who actually believe that it is illegal to interview the accused. This requires a delusional mis-interpretation of the U.S. Constitution. Although the accused has the right *not* to speak to the accuser (whether in a court of law or under any other circumstances), this does not mean that the accused *cannot* speak to the accuser if he or she wishes to. Most accused individuals (especially those who are genuinely innocent) are most eager to confront their accusers. Yet these accused individuals are often deprived of this constitutional right. There are validators who, after interviewing only the child, unashamedly write in their reports that the child was abused and *name* the accused without ever having interviewed or even spoken to him (her).

Generally, these evaluators do not even conduct detailed inquiries with the adult accuser (most often the child's mother). They take at face value her accusations and do not consider the possibility that they may be fabricated or delusional. Rather, they do the opposite, namely, take any shred of information that might support the conclusion and use it in the process of "validation." As mentioned, they will consider normal childhood behaviors as manifestations of sexual abuse, e.g., nightmares, bedwetting, temper tantrums, mood swings, and, of course, masturbation. The mother's report of these occurrences serves to confirm that the child was indeed abused. And the validator becomes even more convinced that the abuse took place, when the child exhibits in the office what are traditionally considered to be psychopathological manifestations. Rather than look into other possible sources of such problems in family life—sources unrelated to sexual abuse—they immediately come to the conclusion that these behavioral difficulties are the direct result of the sex abuse. (As mentioned, every symptom in the diagnostic manual has been listed as a possible result of sex abuse. Accordingly, everything now fits together and the abuse is "validated.")

There are a many ways in which interviewing the accused could be useful in such evaluations. These not only involve interviewing the accused alone, but also interviewing the accused in joint sessions with the accuser, the alleged victim, and all three together. This is the best method for "smoking out" the truth. Family therapists know this well, but these examiners seem to be oblivious to this obviously useful technique. The argument that the child might be traumatized by such a confrontation is not an excuse to preclude its utilization entirely. First, examiners should have the freedom to decide whether or not such joint interviews would do more good than harm. By automatically precluding involvement with the accused, this option is not utilized. Furthermore, although such confrontations may be psychologically traumatic to the child under certain circumstances, one must also consider the psychological trauma to the person falsely accused. It can result in a completely ruined life and/or years of incarceration. These rights of the accused are rarely considered by these examiners. On many occasions I have been asked to interview a child—and only the child—and then make a decision regarding whether or not the child has been sexually abused. I have *never* accepted such an invitation. Before involvement in the case I make every attempt to obtain a court order in which all three parties are required to participate (the accuser, the accused, and the alleged victim), individually and in any combination that I consider warranted. This does not automatically involve a joint interview with the alleged victim and the accused, but it often may. In either case, I must be given the freedom to make that decision.

WHY DO THESE PEOPLE DO IT?

Obviously, there are a wide variety of individuals who serve as validators. Equally obvious is the fact that for each person there is a multiplicity of factors operative in this career choice. There are also many factors involved if one is to explain why these individuals function as they do. No one person will fit into all of the categories mentioned below; however, I am convinced that each of these explanations is applicable to at least some of the individuals who serve as validators.

Impaired Educational Background

There is no question that we are witnessing a progressive deterioration of educational standards throughout the United States. Although there are certainly areas in which things have improved in recent years, there is no question that there are more areas in which things have degenerated—so that the overall picture is much more in the direction of downhill than uphill. The erosion of standards has occurred at just about every level, from kindergarten to graduate school. No one can deny that there has been a deterioration in the public schools during the last 25 years, certainly in the large cities and probably in suburban and rural communities as well. One compelling verification of this (if one needs it) is the progressive deterioration of Scholastic Aptitude Test (SAT) scores. But the numbers here do not reflect the full story. The test has progressively become easier. Accordingly, if the test were as rigorous as it was in the past, the deterioration would become even more apparent. Here I will discuss what I consider to be some of the important factors operative in bringing about this deplorable situation, factors at the elementary, high school, and college levels.

Elementary Schools

"All Men Are Created Equal" Ours is seemingly an egalitarian educational system that assumes "all children are created equal" and all children should receive the same educational exposure. This is misguided egalitarianism. The principle blinds itself to the obvious intellectual differences that children exhibit from the time of birth. On the one hand, educators appreciate that every intelligence test has its distribution curve, from the intellectually impaired to the superior. On the other hand, our educational system in the United States does not properly accommodate these differences. I do not claim that there is no appreciation at all of these differences; I only claim that educators do not exhibit enough appreciation of these differences. Although there are special classes for learning-disabled children and technical high schools for those who are not academically inclined, the main thrust and orientation of our educational system is toward preparing youngsters to enter colleges and universities. The ideal presented is that all children should go to college and those who do not achieve this lofty goal bring shame upon themselves and their families.

Most countries have no problem accepting the fact that not all children should be on a strong academic track. Accordingly, in many countries, somewhere between the ages of nine and eleven, children are divided into three tracks. The highest track ultimately leads to the university. The lowest track ends formal, intense academic training at about age eleven or twelve and then emphasizes various trades and skills. And the middle track is somewhere between the two. Of course, if the child has been placed in the wrong track, there is still a possibility of switching. We would do well in the United States to institute such a system. It would protect many children from significant grief. To say that all people should be *treated* equally before the *law* is certainly reasonable. But to say that all are *created* equal is absurd. What is more reasonable to say, as Orwell did in *Animal Farm,* is that "some are more equal than others." Because public statements of such inegalitarianism are considered undemocratic in our society at this time, it is extremely unlikely that such changes will be introduced into our system in the foreseeable future—certainly not before the end of this century.

Some Causes of School Deterioration   Many factors have contributed to school deterioration in recent years. One relates to teachers' salaries. It is unreasonable to expect that schools can attract high-quality, well-educated individuals when other careers provide much greater pay. In most municipalities garbage men make as much as, if not more than, elementary school teachers. The public sector can generally afford to provide higher salaries than private and parochial schools; yet the public schools seem to be getting the poorest-quality teachers. The more dedicated teachers are willing to take positions for lower salaries in order to work in the more academically stimulating atmosphere of the private and/or parochial schools.

I believe there has been a general diminution in the commitment of teachers to the educational process. I am not claiming that this is true of all teachers, only that the percentage of teachers who are deeply committed to their profession has been sharply reduced in the last 15 to 20 years. One manifestation of this trend is the decreased frequency with which children are required to do homework. Giving children homework most often involves homework for the teacher. And less dedicated teachers are not willing to take on this extra responsibility. In previous years there were many more teachers who were viewed to be somewhat hard nosed and dictatorial, yet their despotism was benevolent and years later their students were able to look back with gratitude on what they were "forced" to do. These days, "respect" for the child often involves a degree of permissiveness and indulgence that serves children ill in the course of their education. A good educational experience helps the child learn that there are times when one has to do things that may be unpleasant in order to derive future benefits. "Respecting" the child's wish not to endure such discomforts is basically not in the child's best interests. True respect for children involves the *requirement* that they do what is best for them, not the indulgence of their avoidance of reasonable responsibilities. The net result of these unfortunate trends is that children learn less during their primary and secondary school years—with the subsequent result that SAT scores have dropped significantly during the last 15 to 20 years, and many studies have demonstrated that the majority of children are abysmally ignorant of basic facts about history, geography, literature, English, and mathematics.

Another factor operative in the deterioration of the educational system has been the growth of a generation of teachers who themselves have not learned very much during their own educational processes. Often, these are teachers who went to college during the 1960s, when students' self-indulgence may have reached an all-time high. Grammar, punctuation, spelling, and foreign languages were dismissed as "irrelevant." Many other subjects that required self-discipline and hard work were also often viewed as irrelevant. Graduates of this era are now teaching our youngsters. Not only do many of these teachers serve as poor models for their students, due to their impaired commitment to the educational process, but they are compromised as well in what they can teach. I routinely ask parents to bring in my child patients' report cards. Often I see egregious errors in grammar, punctuation, and spelling. I have had secretaries whom I have had to let go after a week or two because of their ignorance of basic English. They were not people who I felt needed time to adjust to a new job; rather, it might have taken years to get them to reach the point where they could function adequately in a standard secretarial position. They often did not even appreciate how ignorant they were. They did not even recognize that a misspelled word looked misspelled, and so they had no motivation to consult a dictionary for the correct spelling.

High School

In their book *What Do Our 17-Year-Olds Know?* Ravitch and Finn (1987) report a study conducted with approximately 18,000 17-year-olds who were selected to reflect the make-up of the population as a whole regarding region, sex, race, type of school, and type of community. Some of their findings: Thirty percent of the students did not know that Christopher Columbus reached the New World before 1750. More than 35 percent were not aware that the Watergate scandal took place after 1950. More than 30 percent believed that one consequence of the Spanish-American War was the defeat of the Spanish Armada. Approximately half of the students believed that *Nineteen Eighty-Four* dealt with the destruction of the human race in a nuclear war. Over one-third did not know that Aesop wrote fables. Over 42 percent did not know who Senator Joseph McCarthy was nor for what he became infamous. Seventy percent were unable to identify the Magna Carta. And the book goes on and on with many more examples of the abysmal ignorance of the average American teenager. These findings should not be surprising, considering the kinds of educational programs these youngsters are being provided.

Some parents bring their adolescents for treatment because of poor academic motivation. Many of these youngsters attend schools where the educational standards are low and where they are automatically moved ahead every year and then dropped off the edge of the system when they complete the twelfth grade. Some, however, are in more demanding high schools, but they still have little commitment to the educational process. Sometimes the youngster's lack of motivation is indeed related to intrafamilial and intrapsychic problems. At other times, the youngster is merely one of a stream of hundreds of thousands who are moving along an educational track that demands little and provides even less. Their teachers are uncommitted and unmotivated, watch the clock, do not give homework (homework for the student is homework for the teacher), and so do not provide models for their students— models of people who are "turned on" by learning.

College

I believe that *most* (but certainly not *all*) colleges in the United States are not serving primarily as educational institutions; rather, they are serving as what I call "winter camps" that alternate with their students' summer recreational (and sometimes work) programs. Most youngsters attending colleges are not really looking for an education, but for another four years of self-indulgence and prolongation of their dependent state. We have a unique disease in the United States, a disease I call *the college disease*. Millions of parents believe that it is crucial that their children attend college. They actually believe that the schools to which they are sending their children are actually serving educational purposes. When there is a demand for something there will always be individuals who will be pleased to provide a supply of the item, especially when there is good money to be made in the business. Most college institutions in the United States are basically businesses that cater to a gullible population of parents who believe that it is *crucial* that their children (no matter how simple and/or academically unmotivated) have a college education (no matter how specious and inferior).

These institutions have their academic hierarchy, their assistant professors, associate professors, and full professors. They have their college-style buildings (especially red brick and ivy), their alumni associations, their football teams, and their fund-raising campaigns. And they even offer formal courses; the "students" take examinations; and grades are given. Yet the whole thing does not add up to what can justifiably be referred to as an education. The majority of students are not there to learn; rather they are there primarily to have a good time—which often includes significant indulgence in sex, alcohol, and drugs. What they most often learn are some new sexual techniques, what their tolerance for alcohol is, and perhaps the use of some new drugs that they haven't tried before. They also learn how easy it is to get a college diploma. When the "students" are not engaged in these activities, they go through the motions of attending classes, but little is learned. Grade inflation fosters the delusion that they are learning something and ensures that even those with borderline intelligence will get high grades. Professors are concerned that if they give a student a grade lower than B, then the youngster will have trouble getting into graduate school and the college's reputation and popularity may thereby suffer. It is rare for someone to "flunk out." And why should they fail? Does one kick a good customer out of the store? If a customer's parents are willing to continue to pay for the services provided, it would be self-destructive of the college in this highly competitive market to cut off a predictable supply of money because of the student's failure to consume the product being offered.

I am not claiming that *all* the aforementioned criticisms apply to *all* collegiate institutions and *all* students. If I had to give a percentage of those academic institutions in the United States that fit the above description, I would say that it is in the 75 to 80 percent range. As mentioned, these colleges provide many of their students with gratification of pathological dependency needs. Such colleges also serve as a mechanism for transferring dependency from parents to those who administer these institutions. And thwarting college authorities (especially by antisocial behavior and refusal to study) is often a transfer of rebellion from parents to school authorities—a rebellion in which the dependency-denial element is often operative.

When I attended college we generally went from nine a.m. to five p.m. Monday through Friday, and a half day on Saturday. Most courses met four or five times a week and laboratory courses two to three afternoons a week. It was expected that one would do four or five hours of homework a night. School began the day following Labor Day and continued right through early June. There was a one-week Christmas vacation, possibly a one-week Easter vacation, and of course national holidays. Otherwise we went to school. This is no longer the case. Even in the so-called "best" colleges and universities, the formal academic program is far less rigorous. Most students average two or three hours a day of classes while professors may only have to come in five to ten hours a week and are otherwise unseen. These days, the academic year, although it may start around Labor Day, generally ends in early May. Some institutions use the Christmas and/or Easter season as an excuse for an extended holiday (two to four weeks). Others have long vacations (lasting two to four weeks) between semesters. Many need no other excuse for a long break than the season (spring or winter vacation). When I attended college, professors were on campus throughout the course of the day. Things are vastly changed. Today, it is not uncommon for professors to live at significant distances from the campus and appear only on the days when they teach, and often only during the hours when they teach. Otherwise, they are unavailable. Students at these institutions are being short-changed. "Educations" of this kind may cost $15,000 a year or more. Parents and students are being "ripped off."

Recently, a mother of a patient, who teaches at one of the public universities in New York City, related to me an incident that demonstrates well the deterioration of our educational systems, even at the highest level. The woman is a highly intelligent, well-trained, scholarly individual with a Ph.D. in a very demanding field. One day her chairman called her into his office and told her that he was having a problem with her, namely, that too many of her students were failing. He informed her that a 40 percent failure rate was unacceptable. She informed him that she was actually being quite generous, and that if she had graded in a more honest way, about 60 percent of her students would fail. He told her that he had sat in on a couple of her classes, knew exactly what the problem was, and considered it easily rectifiable. He then went on to explain to her that she was not giving tests in the "correct" manner. What she was doing was to tell students on Friday, for example, that there would be a test on Monday covering the material in certain chapters of the textbook. This he considered "unfair" to the students. Rather, the "correct" way to give a test was to tell the students on Friday exactly what questions would be asked on Monday. Under the new system, the failure rate dropped from 40 to 20 percent, but even then she found herself being quite generous. Such procedures are a manifestation of the bastardization of the educational system. They make a farce of education and, worse, are a terrible disservice to students. The next step, of course, is merely to tell what questions will be asked and give the answers that will be expected. If one extends this further, one might as well give out (or sell) the diplomas in advance and save everybody a lot of trouble.

Things are even worse at some of the two-year colleges. Many of these institutions merely go through the motions of providing an education and are basically a sham. Students are given textbooks that are seemingly rigorous and demanding, yet in actuality the students are only required to learn a small fraction of what is presented therein. Those in charge recognize the travesty but are party to it, even at the highest levels. The net result of all this is that students are not getting a bona fide education and are thereby entering into the workplace ill equipped to handle jobs for which they are ostensibly being trained. Also they are being deprived of the feelings of acomplishment and high self-worth enjoyed by those who have acquired skills and talents through years of hard labor and dedication. The situation thereby contributes to psychopathology, because feelings of low self-worth are an important contributing factor in the development of psychogenic symptoms. In addition, such bogus education contributes to psychopathic trends (I am not saying gross psychopathy) because of the sanctions the youngsters are given for "cutting corners," taking short-cuts, and otherwise doing shabby work.

Yet, at the same time that their education is eroding, the

honors that students are receiving become ever easier to acquire. When I graduated from Columbia College in 1952, my recollection is that no more than one percent graduated *summa cum laude,* perhaps another three or four percent *magna cum laude,* and perhaps another five percent *cum laude.* My recollection is that students below the 10 percent level of the class could not hope to acquire any of these honors. In the mid-1980s I attended the Harvard College graduation of one of my children. I noted that the upper 75 percent of the class received one of these honors. In other words, a person could be in the 75th percentile level of the class and would graduate *cum laude.* When I spoke to faculty people about this, I was informed that the school is well aware of its liberal view with regard to bestowing these honors, but that it is justified because it helps graduates get into graduate school and jobs. I am dubious. Those who make these decisions are well aware that cum laude may very well indicate the 50th to 75th percentile of the class and will act accordingly. It serves to compromise the respect for the honor and does Harvard (and other schools who do the same) a disservice. It is one example of the intellectual and moral erosion that has taken place, even at the highest levels of education.

The Education of Validators

People who work as validators are products of this eroded educational system, at all levels, and this weakness in their educational foundation is reflected in their work. A good education, if anything, should provide individuals with "common sense." Validators, above all, lack common sense. In fact, I consider that to be the number one item on the list of their deficiencies. One has to lack common sense if one is to believe the preposterous things that they accept as valid in order to justify their conclusions. There was a time when one had to be bright in order to get into most colleges. As mentioned, this is less often the case today and there are, without question, many validators who are not particularly intelligent—even though they may have a college and/or university education. People who are less intelligent are less likely to have common sense. However, sometimes this can be rectified (to some extent) by academic work that focuses on the capacity for logical reasoning. Courses in logic, mathematics, physics, and chemistry can most likely do this (for those who are intellectually competent to handle these disciplines). In a less direct way, just about any good college course (including the arts) should involve a certain amount of logical thinking. What is clear is that many of these validators lack the basic intelligence and/or the educational exposure that might have provided them with common sense.

When I was in medical school, our professors would frequently say to us: "Remember this: The most likely things are most likely." At first, I thought the warning was both inane and unnecessary. As time went on, however, I came to appreciate the great wisdom in this seemingly absurd statement. The admonition was most often applied to situations in which a medical student would diagnose a patient as having the rare tropical disease that had just been read about the previous night. This was often done in a state of exultation associated with the pride at having made such a brilliant diagnosis. The professor, often trying to avoid putting the student down, would say something along these lines: "It looks like common viral gastroenteritis to me" or "It looks like the garden variety of bacterial pneumonia to me." The reality of the world is that the most common things *are* most common and that one does well to remember this. Validators seem to be oblivious to this ancient and obvious wisdom. Rather, they go in the opposite direction and consider as valid the most unlikely and even prepos- terous possibilities. One does not need a Ph.D. in advanced mathematics to recognize that the likelihood of a nursery school teacher undressing 50 three-year-old children (in order to involve them when naked in a sex orgy), and then dressing them all quickly, is not very likely to end up with every child wearing the exact same socks, shoes, underwear, dresses, pants, shirts, hats, and coats as they came in with.

Every parent knows that the best way to get a three-year-old child to say something to another person is to preface the message with: "I want to tell you a secret and I want you to promise me that you'll *never* tell anyone." This is the most predictable way to get the message into the pool of public information. Yet, these examiners believe that one can do this with a whole class of children and be confident that they will never breathe a word of their experiences to their parents or anyone else. There are three classes of people who believe that one can accomplish this goal of group secrecy by three-year-olds: (1) psychotics, (2) retardates, and (3) zealous validators. The rest of the world well appreciates that it is unreasonable to expect three-year-old children to involve themselves in conspiracies of silence, especially with regard to dramatic experiences (such as people dressed as clowns, monsters, etc., to engaging the children in sexual intercourse, putting swords up their rectums, and feeding them feces). These examiners do not seem to appreciate that it is not very likely that one can feed feces to a group of children, make them drink their urine, and expose them to a variety of other painful and frightening indignities and yet, only minutes later, get them to skip happily out of the classroom without a speck of feces on their lips or a drop or urine on their tongues. When presented with this argument, validators claim that the children have been frightened into secrecy by threats of body mutilation, murder, etc. This too is an absurd rationalization. Let us forget, for the moment, the failure to find these mutilated bodies with which the children were threatened. The idea that the *whole* group could be frightened into silence is absurd. Perhaps a few, but not *all* of them for the extended period between the alleged abuse and its divulgence. In fact, one could argue that frightened children would be even more likely to reveal quickly what they have been allegedly exposed to.

The "Holier-Than-Thou" Phenomenon

Many readers, I would guess, have seen the common bumper sticker: "I brake for animals." There is a "holier-than-thou" message being transmitted here. The implication here is that the driver of the vehicle bearing this message is a kind of individual who stops for animals and that others are less likely to do so. The message communicates to the reader in the car behind that he (she) should be ever on the alert for a sudden stop by the car ahead and that the driver in front is likely to be stopping short quite frequently. "Keep your foot close to the brakes," it says, "because you never know when you'll have to stop short. You don't have to worry about this when you follow other cars, because they're not driven by the kinds of deeply caring people who are sensitive enough to brake for animals.'' I have had the thought that, if I had the opportunity, I would ask such individuals if they brake for human beings. The same phenomenon is exhibited by politicians who claim proudly and sanctimoniously that they are fighting for the homeless, the elderly, the poor, and children who are abandoned. The implication is that their opponents are against these individuals.

Validators often manifest this patronizing attitude. They—unlike the rest of us—are there to protect children. They— unlike the rest of us—''believe the children.'' The implication here is that those who do not believe the children (like the author) are somehow low-life characters who are exposing children to the sea of abusers, who are ever ready to pounce on their prey. It provides these examiners with a feeling of special importance, which likely serves to compensate for basic feelings of inadequacy. If one basically feels competent about oneself, if one basically has a strong sense of self-worth, one does not have to go around looking down one's nose at others. One does not have to go around putting up signs, waving banners, and exhorting one's superiority over others.

The same phenomenon, in a more subtle way, is exhibited by many clinicians in the mental health professions who pride themselves on their ''respect'' for children. They, unlike the rest of us, are *really* sensitive to children's thoughts and feelings. They, unlike the rest of us, *listen very carefully* to what children are saying and have the *deepest respect* for their wishes. In the precious atmosphere of their offices, they provide the child with ''unconditional positive regard'' and reflexly ''respect'' every thought (no matter how outlandish) and every feeling (no matter how at variance with reality) that teachers, parents, and other insensitive individuals do not provide. These same ''therapists'' may reflexly support the child's position in any difference he (she) may have with the parents, again in the service of respecting the child's position. When this attitude on the therapist's part is carried into a sex abuse evaluation, it contributes to the development of false sex abuse accusations. And, when carried over into the treatment of a child who is not sexually abused, it can contribute to the child's delusion

that such an event did occur. Competent and sophisticated therapists know well that true respect for children is not complying with
what they say they want but with what they really need.

I suspect that some readers (especially those whom I have
criticized) would consider me to have exhibited a "holier-than-
thou" attitude throughout the course of this book. I do not deny
that one might easily come to this conclusion. However, in my
defense, I believe that it is important to differentiate two types of
criticism, namely, that which is justified and that which is unjusti-
fied. One could argue that every criticizer is exhibiting a "holier-
than-thou" attitude toward the person being criticized. Whatever
the criticism, no matter how constructive, it has within it the
implicit message that the criticizer is superior to the person being
criticized. The criticizer is basically saying that he (she) acts in a
superior way, knows better, and feels it incumbent upon him (her)
to communicate the corrective measures to the criticized individual
so that he (she) can mend his (her) ways and be a "better person."
And this holds even when the criticism is completely justified and
even when the rectification of the criticized person's deficit(s)
would be a boon to the world. It is important, therefore, to
differentiate between criticisms that are warranted and those that
are unwarranted. People who have bumper stickers saying "I brake
for animals," people who wave the banner "Believe the children,"
and those therapists who proudly proclaim that they "respect"
their child patients are in this second category. People in this
category more justifiably warrant the "holier-than-thou" epithet.
The important question for the reader of this book should not be
whether I warrant the holier-than-thou label, but whether the
criticisms I am making are valid and whether the changes that could
result from their implementation are desirable.

The Erosion of Values

Most would agree that we have witnessed in the last quarter century
a progressive erosion of values in the United States (and probably
Western society at large). Evidence of this deterioration is to be
found everywhere. Crime rates (with isolated exceptions) are ever

soaring. Drug abuse is ubiquitous. Prisons in most states are overcrowded and cannot accommodate the ever-increasing flow of convicted criminals. Many are released into the street before the completion of their sentences in order to accommodate the new wave of inmates. In large cities automobile thefts, muggings, and other "minor crimes" are so commonplace that they receive little if any attention by the police, and the perpetrators rarely are meaningfully punished. Church boxes are pilfered, subway turnstiles are jumped over, garbage is strewn on streets, and human beings evacuate in public. Teachers are ever cutting corners, less homework is given, school vacations are longer, college admission (with rare exception) is easier, and handing in other students' written work ever more common. Plagiarism among faculty people (even in the most prestigious universities) is becoming increasingly commonplace. And the probable increase in genuine child sex abuse in the intrafamilial situation is another example of this psychopathy. (The reader does well not to forget that I believe that bona fide sex abuse does indeed take place and is indeed ubiquitous and may even be on the uprise.)

One of the many manifestations of this moral erosion has been the progressive insensitivity of people to one another. The Golden Rule has essentially become a quaint anachronism. It is all right for clergymen to tell children in Sunday school that they should treat one another as they themselves would like to be treated, but it is another thing to seriously implement this wisdom in the reality of the adult world. Many factors have been operative in producing this state of affairs. Parental modeling plays an important role in children's development of sympathy and empathy (which are directly related to the ability to put oneself in another person's position). The increasing popularity of day-care centers (their value and justification notwithstanding) deprives children of the kind of intimate involvement with biological parents from which values develop. No matter how dedicated the caretakers at these centers, no matter how educated they may be, they cannot provide the same kind of loving concern as a biological parent. (Elsewhere [1988a] I describe this in greater detail, especially with regard to a solution to this problem that would not involve condemning mothers to return to the home to merely cook and change diapers.) Violence on television and in the cinema is ubiquitous. Most often, little or nothing is portrayed about the pain suffered by the victims of such violence. In the 1960s and 1970s, during the days of the "me generation," books that emphasized the point "think of number one" often became best sellers.

Evaluators who conclude that the vast majority (if not all) of the children they see have indeed been sexually abused are likely to have a defect in their capacity to place themselves in the positions of those who suffer from their decision. There is an element of psychopathy apparent in a person who would see a three-year-old child for a few minutes and then write a note stating that a particular individual (the father, the stepfather, a nursery school teacher, etc.) sexually abused that child. It takes a defect in the mechanisms of conscience to do such an abominable thing. One must completely ignore the effects of such a statement on the alleged perpetrator, effects that may include psychological devastation, destruction of one's lifestyle, and years of incarceration. This is what the "me generation" has wrought.

Interestingly, religious fundamentalism is most often (but certainly not always) a manifestation of moral erosion. I recognize that this statement may come as a surprise to some readers, but it is nevertheless a reality. The more the religious fundamentalist attempts to impose his (her) religious beliefs on others, the less sensitivity the religious zealot has for the person being converted. The examples are legion: Christ's crucifixion, the annihilation of the anti-church Albigensian sects in the thirteenth century, the Crusades, the Spanish Inquisition, the numerous religious wars in Europe between the Protestants and the Catholics, and (to skip quickly many such wars and bring us up to the present) the conflicts between the Shiite Moslems and the more moderate Islamic sects. When religious fundamentalism ignores the wishes, ideas, and feelings of other human beings, it is psychopathy masked as religiosity. It is no less a manifestation of moral erosion than the more overt examples cited above. The recent upsurge in religious fundamentalism in the United States may very well be a "backlash" to the "sexual revolution" of the 1960s and 1970s (Miller, 1990). Those in the movement who focus on sex have a convenient vehicle for their condemnation in the form of sex abuse validation. The goal of publicly humiliating and incarcerating every "pervert" can only be reached if there is a significant defect in conscience and a suspension of the very morality that the religious proselytizers and purifiers proclaim to hold in such high esteem.

Sex Abuse Victims

All career choices are determined by psychological factors and even psychopathological factors—and the people who choose sex abuse work are no exception. I believe that people who have been sexually abused themselves in childhood are much more likely to enter this field than those who have not had such childhood experiences. I believe that if one were to compare the frequency of childhood sexual molestation in a thousand sex abuse workers with three to four matched groups of workers in unrelated fields, the percentage of sex abuse workers who were sexually molested as children would be significantly higher than the percentages in the other three to four groups. The sex abuse field is attractive to those who were molested because it provides them with the opportunity for working through in many complex ways residual and unresolved reactions to their early traumas. I am not claiming that these factors necessarily operate at conscious levels (but they may), nor am I claiming that the processes are necessarily pathological (but they may be).

The phenomenon is no different from the factors that operate in just about any other field. To begin with my own field, many people choose medicine because they have grown up in a home with a parent who has suffered with a chronic illness. They may deal with this childhood trauma by devoting their lives to the treatment of others with that particular disorder or to the search for a cure for the parent's illness. Many choose psychiatry or psychology because they hope to gain understanding and even help for their own problems. People who frequently consider themselves to be put upon or victimized may choose law as a vehicle for protecting themselves and others from such persecutions. People who grew up in poverty may aspire to be (and even become) philanthropists; when they give to others they are basically giving to their projected selves. In all of these examples there is a range from the nonpathological to the pathological psychodynamic factors, and each person's balance lies at some point along the continuum.

Among the sex abuse workers who have been sexually molested as children, there are many who use their career experience in healthy ways in their work—much to the benefit of abused children and their families. They have been there, they know what it's like, and they can provide a degree of sympathy and empathy not often possible for one who has never had the experience. But there are others in this group for whom pathological factors are clearly operative in their work with patients—factors that may becloud their objectivity. Some of these individuals harbor significant resentment against the original perpetrator, resentment that may not have been dealt with completely or properly. They vent their pent-up hostility on present-day offenders in a work setting that provides sanctions for such pathological release. And some of these workers operate on the principle that there will never be enough perpetrators to punish, so great is their desire to wreak vengeance on those who sexually molest children. Concluding that an alleged perpetrator is indeed innocent deprives them of their vengeful gratification. It is this subgroup of sex abuse workers who may work with exaggerated zeal to prosecute alleged abusers and resist strongly the idea that some alleged offenders are indeed innocent. They often adhere tenaciously to the position that children *never* fabricate sex abuse. They must blind themselves to the aforementioned developments in recent years that makes this notion an anachronism. Such zeal and denial have contributed significantly to the sex abuse hysteria that we are witnessing at this time.

Furthermore, when these people "treat" sexually abused children, they can gratify vicariously the desire to treat their projected selves. They are curing themselves of the residua of their sex abuse by curing children who have been so afflicted. Again, this may be a normal, healthy mechanism for some who have been genuinely abused. However, if one has to diagnose normal children as being abused and then subject them to years of "treatment," then much psychological damage is being done and such treatment is an abomination. It can destroy children. It can provide chronic psychological trauma. Unfortunately, there are hundreds (and probably thousands) of children in the United States today who are being subjected to such "therapy."

I recognize that there will be some (especially those who work with sexually abused children) who will conclude that what I have just stated is prejudice on my part and that I have no scientific evidence to support my conclusions. I agree that I have no such studies to support my hypothesis and that my conclusions are based on my own experiences as well as colleagues in the mental health professions (some of whom, interestingly, work in the field of sex abuse). My view of people in my own field is no less critical. There is no question that the specialty of psychiatry attracts some of the sickest medical students, and this is no doubt a factor in the reputation we have as being "crazies." This phenomenon also serves as an explanation for the fact that the suicide rate among psychiatrists is the highest of all the medical specialties. Accordingly, if I am prejudiced against sex abuse workers, I may very well be considered to be prejudiced against people in my own field. However, one might also conclude that I am making accurate statements about both fields.

I am not at all claiming that all (or even the majority) of people involved as validators have been sexually abused as children. I am stating only that they are probably more highly represented than other groups in the population of sex abuse workers. There are other psychological factors that may be operative. Involvement in this field provides the various kinds of sexual release described earlier in this book, e.g., vicarious gratification, reaction formation, voyeurism, etc. Many can gratify "savior syndrome" personality qualities. They devote themselves to protecting children from perverts who are to be found everywhere: among divorcing fathers, in nursery schools and day-care centers, in the streets, in parks, and in cruising cars and trucks. It's a dangerous world out there for children, with sex perverts hiding under practically every stone and lurking behind practically every tree. There is much work to be done to protect these children, and these workers have joined an army of heroes who are devoting themselves to their salvation. Is there a more noble way to spend one's life? Can there be a higher cause to which one can devote oneself?

Overzealous Feminists

Although I am basically in sympathy with the aims of the feminist movement, feminists (as is true of all groups) have their share of fanatics. Some of the latter have jumped on the sex abuse band-wagon because it provides a predictable vehicle for venting hostility toward men. These individuals also subscribe strongly (and even fanatically) to the dictum that children never lie and that any allegation of sex abuse must be true. Some of these women were subjected to cruel treatment in childhood by their fathers and other men. Some in this category have generalized from their childhood experiences and assume that all men will be equally abusive to them. Some carry with them a lifelong vendetta and have embarked upon a campaign of vengeance that will involve the destruction of every man who has the misfortune to cross their path and whom they have the opportunity to destroy. These women gravitate toward becoming validators in the same way that iron is attached to a magnet. It is the "perfect" profession for such fanatics. There is a minimum of effort, and with complete social sanction (after all, one is involved in the worthy cause of incarcerating perverts), they can humiliate, destroy, and incarcerate one man after the other in rapid succession.

Monetary Gain

A whole power structure has grown up in which an army of prosecutors, detectives, investigators, and others rely on a continual stream of positive findings and convictions if they are to justify their ever-increasing demands for more funds from legislatures. In the private sector, as well, there is money to be made in the field. I have already mentioned the sea of hungry lawyers who are looking for clients and who are happy to take on any kind of litigation, no matter how preposterous. There is also a sea of hungry mental health professionals (psychiatrists, psychologists, social workers, pastoral counselors, nurse practitioners, family therapists, and a whole group of so-called "therapists") who are happy to have anyone's business, no matter how preposterous the reason for seeking consultation and treatment. Accordingly, there is big money to be made in the diagnosis and treatment of sex abuse. It is indeed a "growth industry." The validators, then, are only one part of this network in which they all need one another if they are to take their share of the money pie that has been made available by a hysterical society to support the system. Many of the validators fear (with justification) losing their jobs if they conclude that too many of the investigated clients are innocent or the charges unsubstantiated.

CONCLUDING COMMENTS

The net result of all of this is that we have here a "no win" situation for individuals accused of sex abuse. In the hands of many of these "validators," no one is innocent. Everyone is found to be guilty. They operate with impunity. False accusers are protected in most states from lawsuits involving slander and libel. I suspect that these "protective" laws are unconstitutional in that they deprive the accused of the opportunity for direct confrontation with the accuser, a right that is provided by the Sixth Amendment of the U.S. Constitution. In many states the accuser does not even have to mention his (her) name to the reporting authorities and will merely be recorded as "anonymous." Yet, an investigation is embarked upon on the basis of the anonymous call, and people have even been jailed as a result of them.

Our founding fathers knew well the terrible indignities and injustices suffered by innocent victims of the European inquisitorial system of adjudication. Hundreds of thousands (and possibly millions) were convicted of crimes they never committed by accusers and witnesses whose identities were unknown to them. It is clear, at least in the realm of child sex abuse accusations, that we have not advanced beyond those horrible times as far as we would like to think. I know of no falsely accused person who has instituted a lawsuit against a government agency that has utilized such anonymous witnesses as a source of information contributing to the individual's conviction. My hope is that such lawsuits will be instituted and that at least one such case will ultimately come to the attention of the U.S. Supreme Court. The use of anonymous witnesses must be unconstitutional.

To the best of my knowledge, malpractice suits against these validators have not been common. We would all be better off if there were some well-publicized malpractice suits against such individuals. Such suits might have a sobering effect on the field. Unfortunately, they are practicing at the same level of competence (more correctly, incompetence) as their peers and so do not satisfy an important criterion for malpractice, namely, that the individual's level of practice is far below what is considered standard for peers at a similar level of training and experience. We are left, then, with a situation in which craziness is considered normality.

Last, I wish to repeat that I recognize that there are many evaluators who are extremely skilled and sensitive and who do not manifest the deficiencies described in this chapter. I recognize, as well, that evaluators, like all other people, exhibit a range of expertise from the most incompetent and defective to the most skilled and insightful. I have focused here on the most common deficiencies exhibited by the most seriously impaired evaluators and am fully appreciative that there are many readers who do not operate at this low level of professional competence. My hope is that readers who react by becoming offended and thereby reject totally all that I say here will reconsider their position and give serious consideration to the possibility that I may be making some important points that may be useful to them. If they can overcome this initial rejection of what I say, they might find here some useful principles and techniques.

7

THE CHILDREN

THE PARENTAL IMPACT PRIOR
TO THE FIRST INTERVIEW

Fear of adult alienation plays an important role in what children feel, think, and do. Children's self-esteem, as well, is very much related to the opinions that adults have of them. Young children operate very much on the principle H.S. Sullivan (Mullahy, 1970) referred to as "reflected appraisals." Having little inner repertoire to utilize as criteria for self-worth by which they can use to judge themselves, they are very much dependent on the appraisals that adults provide them. Accordingly, even prior to the first interview with the evaluator, if a child's parent wishes to believe that the child was sexually abused, the inquiry that such a parent will conduct is likely to be of a form that communicates to the child that the parent expects answers that will confirm that abuse did indeed take place. When one adds children's suggestibility, gullibility, naiveté, and cognitive immaturity, it is quite easy for a parent to elicit comments that will confirm the allegation. In Chapter Five, I described in detail the parental contributions that are likely to affect the child, even prior to the first interview.

CAVEATS REGARDING THE FIRST INTERVIEW

Even the first interviewer will often see a child who has been provided with up-front programming. This is an important point. Sensitive examiners recognize the contamination of previous examiners, especially those of the ilk who use anatomical dolls, leading questions, and other contaminating maneuvers described inChapter Six. But even examiners who consider themselves to be coming in "fresh" may not be able to conduct a "clean" interview because of these earlier contaminations by a programming parent. It is important for the examiners to appreciate the previously described polymorphous perversity of the normal child as well as the input of sexual material from the environment (television, cinema, school prevention programs, etc.). The examiner must also appreciate that memories are not like rocks put in a box, in that they do not just stay there unchanged for all time. Rather, they become distorted, fused, and restructured—especially if significant adults have communicated to the child that they will provide affection if the child verbalizes specific sexual elaborations, but threaten rejection and even punishment if the child fails to provide such verbalizations. The examiner, too, as an adult authority (especially if the examiner's name is preceded by the word "doctor"), is also viewed as a formidable authority. In this setting the examiner has the power to "rework" the child's memories as well. (In Chapter Six, in my discussion of how validators work, I have described the details of this phenomenon.)

CHILDREN ARE LIARS

As mentioned previously in this book, the examiner must appreciate that children *do* lie (even after differentiating between the truth and a lie), that children have delusions, and that lies can become delusions. A number of studies demonstrate well how prone children are to lying. In fact, most people familiar with children consider it normal. Goleman (1988) describes a study conducted by

M. Lewis, a psychiatrist at Rutgers Medical School. Goleman quotes Lewis: "In one study we just completed with three year olds, we set up an attractive toy behind the child's back and tell him not to look at it while we leave the room." (The children are then observed through a one-way mirror.) "About ten percent don't peek while we're gone. Of the rest, a third will admit they peeked, a third will lie and say that they did not peek, and a third will refuse to say." With regard to the third group, Lewis states, "Those who won't answer seem to represent a transition group, who are in the process of learning to lie, but don't do it well yet. They are visibly the most nervous. Those who say they did not look—who lie— looked the most relaxed. They've learned to lie well. There seems to be a certain relief in knowing how to lie effectively." It is reasonable to conclude that the third who refuse to say (who invoke the Fifth Amendment or will not respond until consultation with their attorneys) are also consciously aware of the fact that they are lying. In short, two thirds of the children in this group lied and were consciously aware that they were lying. The examples shown here relate to children's lying in order to avoid embarrassment over disclosure of unacceptable behavior.

But children also lie in an attempt to ingratiate themselves with adult authority. As far back as 1911 Varendock demonstrated this point quite well in two classroom experiments. In one, a group of 19 seven-year-olds were asked a question about a familiar teacher, namely, "What color is Mr. B's beard?" Sixteen replied that his beard was black and two did not provide an answer. The facts were that Mr. B had no beard. In another classroom experiment, 27 eight-year-olds listened to a male teacher talk to the class for five minutes, after which he left. Each child was then asked, "In which hand did Mr. A hold his hat?" Seventeen children said that he held his hat in the right hand. Four stated that it was the left hand. And three stated that he wore no hat. The facts were that he wore no hat. In short, the vast majority of these seven- and eight-year-old children lied. The explanation is not difficult to understand. Children do not enter the world with knowledge of what is going on within it. They are constantly making speculations and guesses in an attempt to understand elements in their environment. They are constantly looking to adult authority to correct their distortions. When the seven-year-olds were asked, "What color is Mr. B's beard?" it is reasonable to assume that many of their thought processes went along these lines: "I don't remember his having a beard. However, the question indicates that he had a beard. So I must have forgotten. I'm always distorting the real world anyway. I don't want to look stupid to the questioner. Therefore, I'll guess and I hope that I'll get the right answer. Black is the most common color for a beard, so I might as well guess black. I hope I'm right." I would speculate also that a similar line of reasoning went through the minds of those who guessed in which hand Mr. A held his hat. They also lie to avoid punishment. When caught fighting, the vast majority of children under nine or ten are going to claim that the other child was the initiator. They lie also to make excuses for themselves, to rationalize inappropriate or unacceptable behavior.

INGRATIATION TO ADULT AUTHORITIES

Children are constantly trying to ingratiate themselves to adults, especially to adults in authority like parents, teachers, and professionals such as physicians, lawyers, and judges. Like all of us, they want to be liked. If lying will serve this end, they are likely to do so. In divorce situations children predictably lie and say to each parent what that parent wants to hear, especially regarding criticisms of the other. This is the most common way they deal with the loyalty conflicts that emerge from divorce and especially from custody disputes. Children embroiled in a custody dispute know where their "bread is buttered." They know that when with parent A, if they express affection for parent B, they may alienate parent A. In contrast, if they join in with parent A, provide criticisms of parent B (new or more ammunition), they will ingratiate themselves to parent A. And the same procedure is used with parent B. The same principle holds when children are being interviewed by validators. They want to ingratiate themselves to them and get the "right answers." If the validator starts with the position that the sex abuse did indeed take place, the child is likely to pick this up quite early in the interview and provide just the responses that the evaluator wants to hear. This tendency of children makes it easy for evaluators to get them to say anything they want. It is almost like taking candy from a baby. Because of the child's naiveté, cognitive immaturity, and suggestibility, the job is made even easier and the child may not realize how preposterous are the statements and testimonials being elicited.

THE KEEPING-UP-WITH-THE-JONESES PHENOMENON

The examiner must appreciate that children in the nursery school setting who allege sex abuse may be doing so as part of the keeping-up-with-the-Joneses phenomenon. After all, if all the other kids are professing sex abuse, why be the only one who doesn't? The others claim that they were at the party where everyone got undressed. The child certainly does not want to admit that he (she) was the only one not invited to that party. The child may initially recognize that there was no such "party," but, after a series of the kinds of coercive interviews described in Chapter Six, may actually come to believe that he (she) did attend. And this is another important point. What originally may have been a fabrication or an idea introduced by another comes to be believed by the child. The fabrication then becomes a delusion. This is a common phenomenon. And these false beliefs may become so deeply entrenched that the child may accept them as valid throughout the course of life.

NOTORIETY

Then there is the element of notoriety. Many of these children are surrounded by an army of people who provide them with significant attention. There are the child protection workers, the lawyers, the psychologists and psychiatrists, the prosecutors, and the judges. Neighborhood people are constantly "buzzing" about the sex abuse scandal that took place in the child's nursery school. The children are pointed to by friends and neighbors as the ones who attend "that" nursery school that we all heard about. Many of these cases are given significant coverage by the public media.

Reporters, TV announcers, and even appearances on television are possible. All this attention can be enormously gratifying to the child, who may recognize, at some level, that if nothing ever happened, then all these people would evaporate and the notoriety would come to an end.

THE PROGRESSIVE ELABORATION
OF THE ACCUSATIONS

There is a typical pattern in the development of these children's sex abuse scenarios. Although they may start at different places, they often end up with similar stories, especially with regard to the introduction of the aforementioned preposterous elements. A child involved in a vicious custody dispute may begin with a scenario involving the father's touching the child's genitals while taking a bath or shower. In the day-care setting, the usual sequence is for one child to profess molestation and then others to describe similar indignities after initial denial. In the nursery school and day-care settings, the vast majority of children at first deny any abuse. However, with the assistance of the validators and prosecutors they are helped to "remember" and then join with their fellow students and provide new and ever more dramatic material for one another's elaborations. However, as the hysteria ripples through the school and the parents, validators, and prosecutors jump on the band-wagon; the stories tend to develop in a similar fashion—again in the direction of the utilization of the aforementioned preposterous elements.

While all this is going on there are some children who recognize that they themselves were never abused, even though they have been seduced into alleging such abuse. And they may suspect that this is indeed the case with classmates as well. The older the children, the more likely there will be some in this category. However, they have made their statements and recognize that recanting will involve significant rejection from the professionals, who have made it clear that denial will result in significant criticism and even public humiliation. For these children it is easier to go along with the crowd than to stand up and say that all this is crazy and nothing ever happened. The younger the child, the more difficult it is for the youngster to raise up his (her) head above the sea of hysterical people and claim that all this is crazy and that nothing ever happened. This is especially difficult in a situation where outsiders often take the position: "I don't believe all these absurd stories. However, if all this is going on, *something must have happened*. The idea that *nothing happened* may seem preposterous to the outsider. Such a position by outsiders (including judges and juries) makes it even more difficult to maintain the position of denial or retract the scenarios of false allegations.

Although children who have been genuinely abused have certainly been victimized, those who have been subjected to the kinds of interrogations and validations described herein have also been victimized. In both cases their innocence and naiveté have enabled exploiters to use them for their own personal ends. It is safe to say that both forms of victimization can result in lifelong psychological damage; but it is difficult to know which type produces more trauma—especially because the type of victimization focused on in this book is such a recent phenomenon. As mentioned, I believe that many of these children will forever believe that they were sexually abused and some will become psychotic. If my predictions prove true, then these victims of false accusations will probably end up more traumatized (on the average) than those who have been genuinely abused.

8

PHYSICIANS

We in the medical profession are part of the network of people involved in the sex abuse hysteria. Psychiatrists have become involved as evaluators (we do not call ourselves "validators") and as therapists. Unfortunately, there are psychiatrists whose level of evaluation is no better than the validators described in Chapter Six. Unfortunately, as well, there are psychiatrists who "treat" the children who have been diagnosed by such validators as having been sexually abused. Such psychiatrists accept these people as "experts" and then "treat" the child. It would be an error for the reader to assume that I have any less scorn for these medical colleagues than I do for those in other professions who "treat" children for sex abuse when there is little if any evidence that such abuse took place.

A recent development in the field of psychotherapeutic psychiatry is the "uncovering" of early sex abuse that the patient never realized took place. This has been very much in vogue during the last few years. Sometimes the process starts with the psychiatrist "suspecting" sex abuse on the basis of allegedly derivative statements and symptoms that are "suggestive" of early childhood sex abuse. When the patient expresses puzzlement and even disbelief, he (she) is encouraged to enter into a more meaningful and deeper (sometimes on the couch) therapy in order to "uncover" these lost memories. Human beings, suggestible and gullible animals that we are, are likely to comply with the psychiatrist's prediction and provide the psychiatrist with the "lost" material. Such patients, then, go around the rest of their lives proudly telling others how they learned in their treatment how they were sexually abused as children and that this revelation not only served as an important advance in their treatment but brought about other changes that would not have been possible without the revelation. Some even believe that it was the sex abuse that was at the root of many (if not most) of their problems and that now that it has been brought into conscious awareness, the symptoms that derive from it have been reduced significantly, or even evaporated entirely. Such a statement is testimony to the credulity of the human being. It is patently preposterous if the sex abuse never took place (a likely possibility). However, even if there was sex abuse, it is extremely unlikely that most of the patient's problems were derived from this experience (or even experiences). No symptom is caused by one event or one type of event. Symptoms are multi-determined. Furthermore, insight is only one small part of the therapeutic process. Such scenarios may make good movies and novels and may make the author a lot of money, but they have nothing to do with real therapy as it takes place in the real world.

Interestingly, an even *more* recent development is the suspicion by patients—arising within themselves—that they *may* have been sexually abused and were not aware of it. Here, it was not the therapist who suggested this possibility, but the patient. Like all phenomena, this phenomenon has multiple determinants that vary with each individual. Perhaps some of the people actually were sexually abused and the therapeutic inquiry is warranted. Others, I am certain, were never abused but may be looking for a simple answer to explain their problems and, by implication, a magical solution to their difficulties. Others, I am certain, are just keeping up with the Joneses and have been affected by the mass hysteria phenomenon.

Physicians in other branches of medicine have also become deeply involved. This is especially the case for pediatricians, pediatric gynecologists, and people from other branches of medicine (such as internal medicine and family practice) who have become "experts" on sex abuse in recent years. Those who diagnose sex abuse in the vast majority of cases presented to them are generally attractive to prosecutors, who can rely upon them to provide the "definitive medical evidence" that is the "proof" that sex abuse took place. Those who rarely find sex abuse are likely to be engaged by defense attorneys in order for them to testify that the child is "normal" and that there was "no evidence for sex abuse." Although there are people who claim that they are completely neutral, my experience has been that most people who are doing this kind of work have a reputation (whether warranted or not) for being in either of the two camps.

There are doctors (even pediatricians) who claim that any inflammation of a little girl's vulva is a manifestation of sex abuse. Most, however, claim that this is an extremely common finding and can result from sweat, tight pants, certain kinds of soap, and the occasional mild rubbing (and masturbatory) activity of the normal girl. There are some who hold that the normal hymen is a perfect circle (or close to it) without any irregularities. It follows, then, that if any irregularities are found, these must have been artificially created by the insertion of something, possibly a finger, possibly a penis, or possibly something else (like a crayon or pencil). There are others who claim that the normal hymen is most often not a circle and there are irregularities, tags, and bumps. Others hold that these irregularities (referred to as a serrated hymenal orifice) are within the normal range of hymenal variation (I am in agreement with this group). Some claim that a three-year-old girl's vagina can accommodate an adult's fingers and even penis without necessarily showing signs of physical trauma, other than the production of the aforementioned irregularities, tags, and bumps. Others claim that the insertion of an adult male penis into a three-year-old girl's vagina will produce severe pain, significant bleeding, and deep lacerations, and that the insertion of crayons and pencils at that age is extremely rare because of the pain and trauma that such insertion will produce (again, I am in agreement with this group).

There are significant differences of opinion regarding what is the normal size of the hymenal opening, and this, of course, bears directly on the question of abuse. Most agree that there have not been large studies of many children at different ages with regard to what the normal hymen looks like, its size, and whether or not it is indeed circular. Furthermore, all do agree that the older the child, the greater the likelihood the vaginal opening will accommodate a penis without significant trauma; and so that by the age of nine or ten one does not get the same degree of trauma that one may get at younger ages. Most agree, as well, that children of nine and ten, whose vaginal orifices are still small, could still be brought to the point of intercourse with an adult by gradual stretching of the vagina in the course of repeated experiences in which progressively larger objects (fingers, and ultimately a penis) are inserted. There are some who hold that a certain type of dilitation ("winking") of the anal mucosa is pathognomonic of penile penetration into the anus. There are others who claim that such dilitation is normal (again, I am with the group that holds that the puckering described here is most often normal and is not a manifestation of sex abuse).

The net result of this is that there are sharply divided opinions among physicians regarding whether a particular child has been sexually abused. However, this does not stop each side from bringing in a parade of its own physicians who predictably provide the "proof" or "no proof" findings that are requested. Another result is that many doctors are making a lot of money, especially because providing court testimony can be quite remunerative. Wakefield and Underwager (1987) provide a comprehensive review of the literature on the present status of medical findings in sex abuse evaluations.

9

PROSECUTORS

Prosecutors, like other professionals, exhibit a wide range of skill, from the highest to the lowest. I focus here on those who have contributed to the sex abuse hysteria described in this book. I recognize fully that there certainly are prosecutors who are not in the category described here; but there are enough in this reprehensible category to warrant my comments.

When a prosecutor concludes that no sex abuse has taken place, he (she) will enjoy little public attention. After all, there is nothing to talk about when the conclusion is that there is "no evidence." In contrast, if the prosecutor finds that there is "suggestive evidence" (no matter how remote and preposterous), then there is "much work to be done." The uncovering process (often with justification referred to as a "witch hunt") demands significant attention as interested parties (and they are everywhere) eagerly await the outcome of the investigation. All the details need be divulged if one is to have "a good case." Every remnant of sexual behavior must be "dug up." In the process of the investigation, the prosecutor can gratify the same sexual urges described previously for the validators (vicarious gratification, reaction formation, voyeurism, etc.). But these benefits are intrapsychic and certainly do not provide notoriety. A young prosecutor, with no particular standing in the community, has an opportunity here to make a name for himself (herself). Other forms of investigation attract little attention in the public media or, at most, may receive occasional attention in the back pages of the newspaper (with the exception of murder cases, especially "juicy" ones). Sex abuse cases in nursery schools and day-care centers make headlines. What a wonderful opportunity for a young prosecutor "on the way up." It is an opportunity for overnight fame. Typically, these prosecutors work closely with parents, and it behooves them to intensify the hysteria in order to ensure their continually being in the public eye. The prosecutor becomes viewed as the hero who is protecting innocent children from perverts—certainly a noble calling.

A prosecutor is basically a civil servant. It is a salaried position with the usual increments. In the crowded field of law today, the "best and the brightest" generally take jobs with prestigious law firms (sometimes after a year or two of "internship" with judges in high-level positions). Idealistic ones will often gravitate (usually for only a few years) to legal aid and other low paying positions, through which they can gratify their humanitarian inclinations. Civil service jobs are generally not those sought after by the superior students. Rather, they are more likely to be taken by those who have been less successful academically. This intellectual impairment is an asset when one is working as a prosecutor in sex abuse cases. It enables one to believe some of the preposterous things that they are told by the validators and thereby enables them to stay in the system and enjoy the benefits to be derived from such involvement. Other prosecutors, of course, are not justifiably placed in this category. They may be quite intelligent, but gravitate toward the work for other reasons—such as the potential for notoriety and the opportunity to gratify (in a socially approved way) sadistic urges via the deep involvement with criminal elements that the work entails.

In some cases, the prosecutor may have established a reputation as being in the Casey-always-gets-his-man category. Once Casey concludes that the alleged perpetrator is guilty, he never lets go. He will carry it up to the Supreme Court if necessary. Nobody escapes Casey once he is convinced that the crime has been committed (and Casey is easily convinced). He would like to maintain his "perfect record" in order to ensure his reputation as "one of the best, if not *the* best." And the parents feel grateful that they have been lucky enough to have an individual of Casey's reputation on the case. So Casey gets his fame, promotion, and higher salary; the accused goes to jail. Casey deserves everything he got for his efforts; the perverted perpetrator deserves what he got for his perversity.

10

JUDGES

There was a time when many people became judges because it was viewed by the legal profession as a "high calling." The scholarly types gravitated toward the field, especially those who had a high sense of ethics and values and were willing to suffer financial privation in the service of performing this important work. There were others, however, for whom other reasons were operative. Many were attracted to the enormous power that judges wield. For many this could serve as excellent compensation for feelings of inadequacy. The whole courtroom performance provides such gratifications. The judge, in robes, enters the courtroom and everyone stands silently, presumably in deference. From the bench everyone in the courtroom "snaps to"; anyone who dares to openly defy the judge may be put in jail. Of course, these two extremes do not exist in isolation and for many people in the field there was and is probably a combination of both sets of factors. Of course, there are other factors operative in this choice of professions (as is true of any kind of work). The judge enjoys esteem outside the courtroom. Although people are not required to "kowtow," they often do so even though the judge has no jurisdiction over anyone outside the courtroom. A judgeship can be a political plum provided for service to the party. If elected, it can be a statement about the judge's popularity with members of the community. And, at the highest levels, it can be a source of enormous prestige. It can also be a civil service job for people who could not be successful in private practice, a judgeship providing this group with a secure niche and predictable salary increments.

In recent years I believe there has been a shift toward more opportunists and incompetents entering the field, and fewer idealists. I suspect that, at this point, there are still many idealists, especially at the highest levels, but I am convinced that the opportunists, incompetents, and those with less noble motives are very much on the scene. It would be an error for the reader to conclude that I view judges to be a lower breed than people in other disciplines and professions. Every field has its range from the most dedicated and skilled to the most incompetent and ignorant. There are judges who are not taken in by the hysterical parents, coercive validators, opportunistic prosecutors, and the others who parade before them in these cases. (Their cases do not attract much attention in the public media.) But there are so many judges who believe these people that we have a national scandal.

There is nothing in the U.S. Constitution that requires a judge to be a lawyer. Although most do have legal training, it is not a requirement of the office. Obviously, most would consider it desirable that the person at least be a lawyer. Judges are either elected or appointed. Those who are elected must ever concern themselves with their reputations, or else they might not be reelected. And those who are appointed must consider those who have appointed them. The appointments are often made along the lines of political parties, and often influential individuals in the party play an important role in their appointment. And political parties are also very much concerned with their reputations. Accordingly, judges are very much in the public eye and recognize that unfavorable press may jeopardize their positions, whether it be for reelection or reappointment.

A judge who has a reputation for protecting us from perverts, who puts them behind bars if there is even the slightest suspicion that they have sexually abused our children, will generally be viewed with approval and gratitude. In contrast, the one who has allowed even one pervert to roam the streets may not be reappointed. Under these circumstances, judges will often take no chances. There are judges who have openly made statement along these lines: "If there is one scintilla of evidence, no matter how remote, that this person sexually abused a child, I will do everything in my power to remove him (her) from society." In the service of this goal, constitutional protections of due process are ignored. The principle of our founding fathers that a man is innocent until proven guilty is basically shelved. In these cases, a man is guilty until proven innocent. The principle that it is preferable that a hundred guilty men be set free than one innocent man be incarcerated is reversed in these cases. The principle that *is* utilized is that it is preferable that a hundred innocent men be found guilty than one guilty person be allowed to go free. Such judges get positive feedback from hysterical parents and thereby enhance the likelihood of reappointment.

Judges are not free from the psychopathological mechanisms described above for parents and validators. They too may have repressed pedophilic impulses over which there is suppression, repression, and guilt. Inquiry into the details of the case provides voyeuristic and vicarious gratifications. The condemnation of the accused serves the purposes of reaction formation. Incarcerating the alleged perpetrator may serve psychologically to obliterate the judge's own projected pedophilic impulses. At the time I write this (1990), I believe that judges are becoming increasingly aware of the perversity of what is going on in the sex abuse scene and are less prone to believe some of the preposterous scenarios that are being presented to them in court. My hope is that this trend will continue, so that we will ultimately look back upon this period as one of the "crazy times" in our society, similar to that which occurred at the time of the Salem witch trials.

11

LAWYERS

Much money has been made in child sex abuse cases by lawyers. Lieberman (1983) describes what he considers to be the factors operative in this phenomenon. With a ratio of approximately one lawyer for every 345 people in the U.S. population (1989 figures), it is not surprising that there are many "hungry" lawyers. Hungry lawyers can rely on hysterical parents, validators, and prosecutors to keep the hysterical fires burning. Recently, I saw on television a program about a case in Texas in which child sex abuse was alleged in a day-care center. Lawyers literally swarmed to the homes of children who had not professed sex abuse and tried to convince parents that their children probably had been abused and that such abuse could be "proven" if only they were to be evaluated by a properly trained validator (whom the lawyers would be happy to refer). The parents were also advised that there was much money to be made in the subsequent lawsuits. Unfortunately, the gullibility and the greed of these parents caused many of them to allow themselves to be drawn into this sordid scheme. Their gullibility and greed resulted in their denying the devastating psychological effects on their children of being dragged through the offices of validators, prosecutors, lawyers, mental health professionals, and then subjected to years of "treatment."

Again there are some lawyers who indeed do not warrent such harsh criticism. They may genuinely believe that the children they are representing have actually been abused. They are honest and have deep conviction for their position. I, however, view them to be unsophisticated with regard to the criteria one should be utilizing when deciding whether a child client has been genuinely abused. I have met many in this category who are indeed very eager to learn. Some have been so swept up in the hysteria that they may no longer exhibit the objectivity they manifested in other cases previously. For some, involvement provides the same kinds of pathological gratifications described previously for the other professionals who gravitate toward this field, e.g. vicarious pedophilic gratification, voyeurism, etc.

12

THE SO-CALLED
THERAPISTS

We are continually being told that there are so many children being sexually abused these days that we do not know where we are going to get all the evaluators to examine them. And all these children are going to need years and years of intensive "therapy" if we are ever to hope to cure them of the symptoms that have been derived from the terrible psychological traumas to which they have been subjected. And this is going to cost lots and lots of money.

It is important for the reader to appreciate that there is no formal certification required of anyone who wishes to be a "therapist." There are requirements to be a psychiatrist, clinical psychologist, and psychiatric social worker. In many states there are standards for family therapists, pastoral counselors, and nurse practitioners. All of these groups share in common the label *therapists*. However, anyone can put up a sign saying that he (she) is a therapist and cannot be run out of town with the claim that the individual is "practicing without a license." It is not surprising that, with the tremendous need for therapists for these sexually abused children, many have come to jump on the bandwagon and fill the vacuum. These therapists hold meetings describing to parents the need for therapy and appeal to their guilt and gullibility in the course of such presentations. They predict dire consequences for children who do not enjoy the benefits of the therapist's treatment, which again is necessarily going to be quite long and expensive.

What is being ignored is the psychological trauma *caused* by the so-called "treatment," which in itself is causing the problems— problems that may be lifelong. In the course of such "therapy" children are taught to be ever vigilant for sex abuse perpetrators. The treatment engenders distrust of even one's closest relatives. It brings about a paranoid attitude about the world in which sex abuse perpetrators are ubiquitous, cunning, and dangerous. Particularly devastating is the effect of such treatment on the child's relationship with the father, if he is the alleged perpetrator. Whether the father is actually guilty or genuinely innocent, the therapist works on the assumption that the father has indeed been guilty. Accordingly, the therapeutic approach involves venting anger toward the father (hitting Bozo dolls and other presumably therapeutic methods for releasing pent-up hostility) and helping the child gain mechanisms for being protected from future sexual advances and coercions. The notions of rapprochement and possible correction of the father– child relationship generally are not included as part of the thera- peutic process. In many cases the parent and child are separated for long periods, and sometimes permanently. This usually involves the father's removal from the home by court order. However, in some cases it is the child who is removed from the home, especially if the mother is deemed to be someone who could not properly protect the child from the abuse.

Another serious problem that results from such therapy is that the child's capacity to differentiate between fact and fantasy becomes seriously compromised. At the outset, the child is brought to believe that sex abuse occurred when, in fact, there was no such experience. But things do not stop there. Typically the therapist is successful in progressively "uncovering" more details that presum- ably have been repressed and now (as a result of the therapist's skill) are being brought into conscious awareness. The child comes to believe these fantasies (both its own and those projected by the therapist) as well, further distorting the child's capacity to differen- tiate fact from fantasy. I believe that many of the children who are being subjected to this kind of treatment will end up psychotic. And this is especially the case for those whose treatment begins early in life (such as at the age of two-and-a-half to three) and extends over a long period. Most of the children receiving such therapy at this time are considered to be so severely damaged by their sex abuse that the therapy is expected to take many years. In fact, I have not yet seen one case in which the therapy has been completed, so deep seated is the psychological trauma said to be. Of course, my prediction that many of these children will ultimately become psychotic cannot yet be verified, because their treatment has only been going on for less than a decade. I am convinced that follow-up studies of these children will verify what I have stated here.

All this is tragic for these families, with the exception of those cases in which there is genuine abuse from which the child cannot be protected. However, there are many cases of bona fide abuse in which less drastic measures can be utilized, especially measures involving rapprochement with the abuser, but these are rarely utilized. When, however, the abuse never took place, then this therapeutic approach is even more tragic. It brings about alienation from a parent, who in most cases could have provided good parenting. It may result in lifelong rupture of the father–child bond, much to the detriment of both parties. And, unfortunately, this tragedy is taking place daily.

Sexual inhibition problems are also likely to result. These children are taught that sex is bad and dangerous and they are not generally capable of differentiating at that age between pathological and healthy sex. The idea that the child can then be "subsequently straightened out" is a myth. The chronic state of vigilance cannot but contribute to the development of a wide variety of symptoms. Although we have no follow up studies at this point on the children who have been subjected to this "treatment," there is no question that many of them will be damaged for life (and I myself have seen some of them).

I recognize fully that there are many therapists who treat sexually abused children who are highly skilled and competent and do not warrant the criticisms presented here. Therapists, like all other professionals, exhibit a wide range of expertise. But I am not talking about these sensitive and sophisticated therapists here. I am focusing here on those who are far less competent and who have caused significant psychological damage to children and their families. There are enough of these incompetents around to warrant my comments. Therapists in the latter category have played a significant role in the hysteria we are witnessing at this time.

A recent related trend among therapists is the phenomenon of adult psychologists and psychiatrists (especially psychoanalysts) finding evidences for childhood sex abuse in patients with whom they had not previously even suspected such experiences. Under these circumstances they are asked to increase the frequency of their treatment in order to delve even more deeply into their childhood experiences in the hope that divulgence of such will bring about the alleviation of a wide variety of their problems. This phenomenon is testament to the gullibility and suggestibility of the human adult (both the patient's and the "psychoanalyst's") and that suggestibility is not simply confined to children. All of these trends in the mental health professions is reminiscent of the anecdote:

Question: "What's the difference between a neurotic, a psychotic, and a psychiatrist?"

Answer: A neurotic builds castles in the air; a psychotic lives in them; and the psychiatrist collects the rent.

13

SOCIETY

Social factors have been operative in contributing to the mass hysteria that we are witnessing at this time, factors that are operative beyond the home (where the child custody dispute allegations arise) and the school house (where the day-care center and nursery school allegations arise).

EXAGGERATED REACTIONS TO PEDOPHILIA

Shakespeare's *Hamlet* said it well: "There is nothing either good or bad, but thinking makes it so." Our judgments and interpretations of external events are far less related to actual reality than they are to our desires to see things in our own way. Sexual fondling of children (I am not referring here to rape and other forms of physically destructive sexual encounters) is probably an ancient tradition and is to be found in all societies. Societies have differed, however, with regard to their acceptance of pedophilic acts. The aboriginal Hawaiians, for example, practiced noncoercive pedophilia routinely— somewhat to the surprise of the European invaders. (I am not making any personal judgments on these acts; I am just stating the facts.) There is no question that our society is excessively punitive with regard to the punishments we impose on people who are involved in noncoercive sexual encounters.

There are states in which an adult found guilty of touching (and *only* touching) a little girl's vulva may be given a mandatory jail sentence of 25 years or even life imprisonment. There are a wide variety of other crimes these perpetrators could have committed for which they would have been given only a tap on the wrist. Had they stolen money from these children, struck them, told them frightening or preposterous stories, or thrown rocks at their heads, they would not even have been sent to jail. Assault and battery might only result in a suspended sentence and/or probation. In day-care center and nursery school cases, where many children are involved, each case is tried independently and each conviction is added to the previous one. When 20 or 30 children are involved (not uncommon in such cases), the accused faces 20 or 30 life sentences—*consecutively*. More commonly, shorter sentences are given, such as 15 to 20 years, so that the accused may face sentences of 500 to 750 years of imprisonment.

There are many psychological mechanisms operative in what I consider to be society's overreaction to child sex abuse. One such mechanism is reaction formation. Overreaction is the hallmark of this defense mechanism. Many people deal with their unacceptable and repressed sexuality by projecting it outward and then condemning vehemently those who do exactly what they would like to do, but cannot permit themselves to enjoy. And this, of course, is what is going on when we refer to someone as a "pervert," namely, someone who does what we find "disgusting," i.e., who does something that we would like to do; we use revulsion as a method of preventing ourselves from engaging in the activity. Freud in his *Civilization and Its Discontents* (1930) pointed out that society must suppress and repress sexuality if any constructive work is to be done. If all individuals were free to indulge themselves in any form of sexual encounter, we would have little time to involve ourselves in the constructive work necessary for the survival of society.

Accordingly, various mechanisms are called into play to allow for release of the excess sexual energies (that is, those that press for release beyond procreative purposes) in ways that are not detrimental to society. For example, sublimation—that is, allowing release in the form of substitute and symbolic channels—is one such mode of release. Reaction formation allows for fantasy release (by visualizing the activity one is condemning) and, at the same time, enforces the suppressive (conscious) and repressive (unconscious) mental operation. The major problem with this (and other such mechanisms) is finding the degree of suppression and repression that is desirable. Long before Sigmund Freud, many probably appreciated that too much suppression and repression might result in various forms of psychopathology; yet too little utilization of these forces might not be in the best interests of society at large in that constructive work might not then be done. Accordingly, some middle ground had to be found, some level that is neither too repressive nor too permissive. And what is a problem for society at large is often a problem for each of the individuals who make up the group. Most of us are ever dealing with this conflict.

I believe that one of the factors operative in the mass hysteria that we are witnessing at this point relates to the "backlash" reaction to the sexual permissiveness of the 1960s and 1970s. This period of sexual freedom produced a wide variety of reactions in both participants and nonparticipants. I will focus here only on that group of individuals who are excessively moralistic with regard to sexual release and tend to be somewhat punitive toward those who allow themselves such gratifications. Many of these excessively moralistic individuals are secretly envious of those who can guilt-lessly allow themselves such release. They cannot express this directly; in fact, it may be unconscious. In order to protect themselves from the discomforts of their jealousy and the tempta-tion of indulging themselves in the forbidden sexual activities, they embark upon a campaign of denigration, the final goal of which is to expunge entirely those who allow themselves greater freedom of sexual expression. The campaign against pedophilia is one manifes-tation of this backlash movement. Nathan (1990) considers this factor to be operative in the rise of religious fundamentalism that we have witnessed in the last decade and sees a direct link between the increasing popularity of these groups and the "overkill" reactions to pedophilia.

It would be an error for the reader to conclude that I personally support pedophilia. I do not. I personally believe that such behavior is an exploitation of children and introduces them prema-turely into a level of sexual activity that they are not cognitively capable of dealing with appropriately. What I am against is the excessively moralistic and punitive reactions that many members of our society have toward pedophiles. The Draconian punishments meted out to pedophilics go far beyond what I consider to be the gravity of the crime.

Although, as mentioned, pedophilia is widespread and has a longstanding history, I still believe that those who are subjected to it in our society are likely to develop psychiatric problems. It is a form of exploitation of an innocent and defenseless child who is not in a position to appreciate the consequences of the act. It can result in premature involvement in sexual behavior, with all the complications attendant to such early introduction to adult levels of sexual excitation. It can create a pathological tie with the abuser that may then make it difficult for the abused individual to relate in healthier ways to age-appropriate peers. However, we have to develop much more pity than scorn for the pedophile. Our hormones know nothing about the incest taboo; therefore, intrafamilial sexual arousal is probably universal. As mentioned, all of us are polymorphous perverse as infants and there is a bit of pedophilia in every one of us. There is no question that an extremely common reaction to the accused pedophilic is: "There but for the grace of God go I." What, then, the reader may ask, do we do with pedophilics? Although it is beyond the purposes of this book to discuss this in detail, I will outline here a few of my general ideas.

First, we must differentiate between those pedophiles who are living with the child and those who are not. Obviously, it is much easier to remove a perpetrator in the latter category than in the former. With regard to intrafamilial sex abuse, skilled evaluators must ascertain whether or not removal is warranted. One must try to determine whether the parent–child relationship is still salvageable, and whether the pedophilia can be dealt with while the perpetrator is still living in the home. Various therapeutic approaches have been tried, with varying degrees of success. The greatest likelihood of success will occur in those situations in which all pertinent family members are involved, that is, the victim, the perpetrator, the spouse of the pedophile, and even other family members. This is just the opposite of the aforementioned therapeutic approaches, in which the perpetrator is viewed as vile and dangerous and the aim of treatment is to bring about a total cessation of the relationship with the child and the parent perpetrator.

Such evaluators do not seem to appreciate that we all have only two biological parents and that the other five-plus billion people in this world are far less likely to be willing to make the sacrifices and give the love and affection that a biological parent is most often willing to and capable of providing. Removal of such a parent from the home should only be seriously considered after all attempts at treatment of the pedophilia and rapprochement with the family have proven futile. Even then, I would not recommend prison as the first choice of placement. The individual can be ordered by the court to live elsewhere and only visit under supervised circumstances. Repeat offenders, must be removed from society. However, enforced living in some kind of protective residence or work camp is certainly preferable to imprisonment with hardened criminals.

In a sense, fewer problems are present when we deal with the pedophile who has no relationship at all to the child victim. Exclusion is generally without complications to the child. However, we are still left with the question of what to do with such a person. These individuals, too, should be given the opportunity for treatment. If that fails then and only then should some kind of forced incarceration be considered. If imprisonment is deemed warranted, I would recommend that the place of incarceration be more in the category of the minimum security facility, rather than one in which the individual is placed in a setting with hardened criminals. In all cases, I believe that longstanding sentences for first offenses (such as 25 years to life, which is not uncommon) are excessively punitive and probably an abrogation of the perpetrator's right under the Eighth and Fourteenth Amendments to the U.S. Constitution not to be subjected to "cruel and unusual punishment."

Another factor operative in the exaggerated reaction we are seeing with regard to pedophilia relates to our previous denial of the phenomenon. There is no question that many have "looked the other way" and denied what was obvious. Intrafamilial pedophilia (that is, incest) is widespread and, as mentioned, is probably an ancient tradition. Miller (1990) has expressed the view that the pendulum has now shifted to the other extreme. What we have once denied we are now seeing everywhere. And this, of course, is contributing to the mass hysteria that we are witnessing at this time.

So what do we do about this? One of the steps that society must take to deal with the present hysteria is to "come off it" and take a more realistic attitude toward pedophilic behavior. I am not recommending that there be no restrictions and I am certainly not recommending that we should allow children (or anyone else) to be raped. Nor am I even suggesting that there be no protection against children being seduced into nonviolent forms of sexual encounters. I am only suggesting that we take a more humane and less punitive reaction to pedophilia and accept the fact that all of us, to some degree, are pedophilics. We must promulgate the notion (in schools, churches, and in the public media) that most (if not all) of us have pedophilic impulses. We only differ with regard to the degree to which we act on them. We have to lessen guilt over our awareness of our impulses (and reduce thereby the tendency to utilize reaction formation), yet engender enough guilt to deter prone individuals from acting on their pedophilic impulses. We must emphasize the disservice to the child that a pedophilic act involves. We must make the punishment much more humane, especially with regard to the reduction of long jail sentences. I am not claiming to present here a total solution to the problem, but I do believe that these recommendations could prove useful.

PUBLIC MEDIA

The public media (newspapers, magazines, radio, and television) are also playing a role in promulgating the state of mass hysteria. There is very little that one could write about a day-care center or nursery school in which there was no sex abuse. Of course, there are other aspects of the nursery school scene that might warrant an article in a newspaper; but it certainly won't make screaming headlines and is not likely to sell extra copies. A sex abuse exposé is "scandalous" and certainly deserves nothing less than front page headlines. The press also provides the parade of individuals involved in these cases (prosecutors, validators, parents, lawyers, psychologists, etc.) the opportunity for notoriety and feeds, thereby, into the perpetuation of the hysteria. And such publicity is likely to enhance the careers (as well as the pocketbooks) of those given this public attention.

And gossip is important. It serves to fill up the vacuum of many people's lives. It adds spice and excitement to what might be an otherwise dull existence. "I would have never imagined it," say the neighborhood people. "It looked like such a nice, friendly, reputable school and all the while we didn't know what terrible things were going on in there. They sure were clever. They really kept it quiet for a long time. When those kids came out, I never thought that they had just eaten feces, drank urine, and were beaten with whips."

Thousands of newspaper and magazine articles and thousands of hours on television and radio have been devoted to these cases. Dozens of books have already appeared and there are more to come (mine is being added to the pile). The public media, therefore, have gotten their "cut of the pie" and will continue to enjoy greater profits as long as the hysteria is promulgated.

FANATIC FEMINISTS

As mentioned, I am in general sympathy with the feminist movement and believe that women have justifiable complaints over the wide variety of indignities they have suffered in world history. And they are still justified in their attempts to rectify some of the abominations to which they have been subjected. However, feminist groups, like all groups, have their share of fanatics. Some of these operate as if they have a lifelong vendetta against men and will never be satisfied until all of them are destroyed. These zealots have found the sex abuse scene to be a perfect opportunity for the expression of their venom. What better way to wreak vengeance on men than to accuse them of sex abuse. One can never be proven innocent, even though the court of law may find "no evidence." Lives have been wrecked and many men have been incarcerated. All one need do is wave the banner that children never lie, and everything just rolls on from there.

Mention has already been made of the attraction of these

zealots to the ranks of the validators. However, they also are represented in the population of parents who mobilize other parents to join the ranks of the protesters. One might add the obvious question here about why it is that these women are equally vindictive toward *female* alleged perpetrators in nursery schools and day-care centers. The answer relates to the fact that some feminists view all sex to serve as the vehicle for the exploitation of women by men. Accordingly, they condemn its every manifestation in both sexes. Nathan (1990) describes this phenomenon in some detail.

THE ALLEGED DEVIL WORSHIPERS

Another group that has ostensibly jumped on the bandwagon has been the Satan worshipers. I say "ostensibly" because—if we are to believe many of the hysterical parents and what we read in the public media—there is an international conspiracy of devil-worshiping cults that is to be found in practically every city. These people, we are told, are actively infiltrating our society, and nursery schools, and sex abuse rituals are just one manifestation of their nefarious activities. It is they, we are told, who engage in satanic rites in which children are raped with crucifixes, sacrificed in accordance with satanic rituals, smeared with human waste, and forced to observe infant sacrificial rituals. The fact that no proven remnants of any of these activities have ever been found does not seem to discourage the promulgation of this notion. It is common for prosecutors, validators, and/or treating psychologists to call special meetings of parents in which "experts" on Satanism are invited to describe in detail the ways in which devil worshipers work. Because satanic cult sex abusers are so cunning, and because they generally work under the cover of darkness, special instructions are necessary if people are to be properly educated about their devious and dangerous manipulations. In one case in which I was involved, the parents invited an "expert" on satanic cults to do an "investigation" in order to determine whether satanic influences were operative in the day-care center scandal. I would suspect that there are many such experts available who are happy to exploit these gullible parents. Some genuinely believe in what they are doing;

others, I am convinced are sociopaths. In either case, both groups of experts can walk away from town whistling on the way to the bank.

I think it is most likely that the number of people in the United States who actually espouse this religion is minuscule. (Obviously, since they worship in secrecy, in the woods, in cellars, and in other secluded places, it is almost impossible to find out what their exact number is.) Although I believe that their actual number is small, the belief that they exist is widespread. Belief in the actual existence of Satan and the belief that he (as some kind of spirit) is responsible for all this mischief is not of primary importance here. What is important is *the belief that a demonic conspiracy exists* and that devil worshipers are having a direct influence on teachers and children in day-care centers and nursery schools. It is this group, we are told, that causes teachers and school administrators to molest children, especially via the utilization of child sacrifice, feces eating, and other alleged rituals. Those who believe that Satan worshiping is a widespread phenomenon will point to Satanic grafitti, T-shirts, the appearance of special Satanic number sequences, and symbols in otherwise innocuous logos and other printed matter, and claim that these provide proof of the ubiquity of Satanism. They only provide proof of the social utilization of these ideas; they do not provide proof of the actual extent of practicing Satanic cults per se. In short, what we are dealing with here is mass delusion superimposed on mass hysteria.

Unfortunately, there is a segment of the psychiatric and psychological community that harbors this delusion as well, the complete absence of concrete evidence notwithstanding. Some in the psychiatric-psychological community do not actually believe in the devil and, by extension, demonic possession. They do, however, believe that multiple personality disorder is much more widespread than we have previously appreciated, and that some of the people who sexually abuse children suffer with this disorder. The "bad self" unconsciously splits off from the "good self" and engages in the sex abuse, which would be unacceptable behavior to the "good self." Such individuals, according to the theory, may even consider themselves to be possessed by the devil at the time of the abuse. Interviewing such individuals, in a standard interview, is of little value, we are told, because the abuser is not consciously aware that he (she) is a criminal perpetrator. It is only in the hands of one of these skilled experts that the true story is likely to be revealed. Proponents of this theory do not need to subject themselves to the criticism of being devil worshipers; rather, they can view themselves as being "scientific" and utilizing well-established psychological principles.

I believe that in the vast majority of these cases these individuals are stretching a psychological principle in order to apply it to a situation in which it has absolutely no applicability. For many years now psychoanalysts have been using the argument—to which there is no defense—that the patient's denial is merely a psychological mechanism for covering up the truth. The psychoanalyst "knows" what has really gone on and the patient's refusal to accept these realities is a mere manifestation of the power of the repressive forces that can relegate material into the unconscious. According to these examiners, when such alleged perpetrators deny multiple personality phenomena, they are labeled as repressing and suppressing the unacceptable material, and their denial is proof that they are sex abuse perpetrators suffering with a multiple personality disorder. In this way, many people who are genuinely innocent of sex abuse find themselves helpless when the accusing finger of the psychoanalytic psychologist (psychiatrist) is pointed at them.

Satanists, however, make good press—especially for newspapers that are looking for ways to fill up the empty spaces on their pages and who are looking to enhance their circulation. Their alleged rites of mutilating babies and eating them are predictably going to attract readers, in part because such activities gratify the readers' primitive "polymorphous perverse" fantasies.

Although no one has ever found any of the remains of the babies murdered in these rituals—murdered in front of nursery school children—this has not dispelled belief in the devil worshipers' active participation in the nursery school orgies of sex and violence. The recent explanation to explain why we do not see evidence for the murdered babies (many cemeteries have literally been dug up in the search for these remains) is that they were *not buried* (as the children originally stated), but they were *eaten*. This seems to be an acceptable explanation for those who have a strong need to maintain the delusions and keep the sex abuse hysteria going. (However, we are still not left with an explanation about what they did with the bones. Perhaps they were ground up and pulverized in a special machine before being ingested.) Explaining the preposterous with yet another preposterous explanation is the hallmark of these allegations and is a clue—at least to people with common sense—that there are many people involved in nursery school scandals who are living in fantasy land.

ADDITIONAL SOCIAL FACTORS

We are very much a child-oriented society. People from most other countries generally consider Americans to be extremely indulgent of their children. Many years ago, after a visit to the United States, the Duke of Windsor was asked about his impressions of Americans. His response (as closely as I can recall): "The one thing that impressed me most about American parents was the way they obey their children." Psychologists and psychiatrists also are ever telling parents about the importance of "respecting" their children. In therapy, especially, many (if not most) therapists take the position that the child's thoughts, feelings, and desires should be given optimum consideration and often indulgence. The parents are sometimes even viewed as the "enemy." The "believe the children" phenomenon is a natural extension of this philosophy. The "children never lie" dictum is also a derivative of this view of the child. A social attitude of greater incredulity and less "respect" of the verbalization of children would have played a role (admittedly small) in squelching the sex abuse hysteria that we are witnessing.

I suspect, also, that the AIDS epidemic is playing a role in what we are observing here. Mention has been made of the backlash to the sexual permissiveness of the 1960s and 1970s. I believe that the AIDS epidemic has fed into this backlash. Those of a religious orientation tend to view the AIDS epidemic as "punishment" for sexual indulgence, especially for such "perverts" as homosexuals— who they believe deserve this fate. But even those who do not hold these views have been influenced significantly by the AIDS epidemic. It has brought about a general inhibition in sexual freedom because of the fear of contracting this dreaded disease. Such fears have contributed to the sexual backlash that has fueled the reaction formation element operative in the nursery school hysteria. It is one of the factors that justifies the condemnation of sexuality, wherever it may manifest itself.

When there is money to be made, there will always be individuals who will be happy to make some. There will always be psychopathic types around who will be happy to exploit people, especially those who are gullible enough to give their money away—practically for nothing. There are far more psychopathic types around who are happy to exploit gullible people than there are strangers lurking in the woods, just waiting to sexually abuse children on their way home from school. In one nursery school sex abuse case I was involved in recently, an individual who prefaced his name with ''doctor'' was involved with an organization, the purpose of which was to provide protection and justice for children who were sexually abused. His main purpose was to provide diagnostic and therapeutic personnel to validate the sex abuse and then provide treatment. Not surprisingly, he received a significant percentage of the money the parents paid to the group for these services. I do not believe that this man is unique. With such money to be made, it is likely that there are many others, all across the country, who are looking for similar opportunities to make a quick buck.

14

THE SALEM
WITCHCRAFT TRIALS

A HISTORICAL REVIEW

Many have noted the similarity between the hysteria associated with the Salem witchcraft trials in 1692 and that which we are witnessing at the present time. I believe that this comparison is warranted. In fact, the similarities between the two phenomena are almost uncanny.

This summary of the events of that fateful year is based on the descriptions of the trials in Thompson (1982) and Richardson (1983). The events began in the winter of 1691–1692 in Salem Village (now part of Danvers, Massachusetts). Betty Parris, age nine, and her cousin, Abigail Williams, age eleven, spent significant time with the family's West Indian slave, Tituba. There is good reason to believe that Tituba spent long hours with the children telling them stories about voodoo spells and witches. During the cold winter days, the Parris home became the gathering place for other girls who, we have good reason to believe, found Tituba's tales a welcome break in the boredom of the Massachusetts winter. The strict demands of their Calvinist parents provided little opportunity for enjoyable activities to pass the time. Even Christmas was not considered justification for joyous worship, let along revelry.

It was during this period that the children developed highly emotional episodic fits associated with screaming; choking; bizarre body contortions; grimacing; inexplicable physical pains; periodic deafness, blindness, and speechlessness; epilectic-like seizures; unintelligible utterances; and trance-like states. Their father, quite concerned over these strange outbursts, summoned the village physician, Dr. William Griggs. The doctor was unable to find any physical cause for this somewhat mysterious illness and suggested that the girls had fallen under Satan's influence. This was a common explanation for diseases of unknown etiology at that time.

The general consensus was that Satan exercised his power through the intermediaries of witches. Typically, witches assumed the identity of individuals who were known to the afflicted person and would appear in a dream or a vision. Following this "diagnosis" Betty's father enlisted the aid of his church colleagues in the hope that they would help him deal with the wicked spirits who had possessed the girls. By February 1692 the affliction had spread to about a dozen other women. The main symptoms by this time were choking; loss of speech, sight, and hearing; muscle spasms; inability to pray; and "spells" during which they saw vivid and frightening apparitions. These visions were said to pursue the girls, threatening to bite, pinch, pluck, and harm them in other ways.

Community leaders were convened to lead a public day of fasting and prayer and to question the afflicted girls about the identities of those who had caused their strange behavior. At first the girls did not provide the identities of their persecutors. They gradually revealed an ever-growing list of names—including Tituba as well as others in the community who seemed to have been selected almost at random.

On February 29, 1692, Tituba and two other women were arrested and were sent to a Boston jail. The girls, however, continued to accuse other individuals. Then, nonafflicted citizens stepped forward and testified that they too had been personally harmed by these witches, had suffered damages to their crops and livestock, or had received midnight visits from the defendants, the "servants of the devil." By April 1692 the witchcraft epidemic had spread to nearby communities. The senior magistrates, ministers, and even the deputy governor were summoned to Salem in order to preside over the trials. By this time more than 50 persons were accused in the nearby town of Andover. The accusations spread to individuals at every level of society, including John Alden of Boston, a prominent and wealthy fur merchant, who, the girls claimed, was the leader of the Boston group of witches.

By the end of May (after delays because of some legal technicalities), Massachusetts governor William Phips appointed seven distinguished men with knowledge of the law to preside over the trials. Interestingly, none of the judges had formal legal training, but all were experienced magistrates and had reputations for high integrity. Those chosen included Lieutenant Governor William Stoughton of Dorchester (chief justice) and other well-known Massachusetts magistrates.

The formal trials began on June 2, 1692. Between then and September 17, 1692, 27 people were convicted of witchcraft. Nineteen were hanged (the last hangings took place on September 22, 1692), one man (who refused trial by jury) was executed by being pressed to death with heavy stones (he took two days to die), and four died in prison. The convicted were executed by hanging. Paradoxically, those who confessed (such as Tituba) were neither tried nor executed.

Early in the trials there were questions already being raised about the criteria by which the court was deciding that individuals were indeed witches. As early as June 10, one of the judges (Judge Nathaniel Saltonstall) resigned because of dissatisfaction with the proceedings. By October 1692 the girls had accused an ever-expanding number of prominent people, including Judge Nathaniel Saltonstall and Lady Phipps, the wife of the governor. Reverend Increase Mather, then president of Harvard College and the Massachusetts Colony's ambassador to England, was deeply disturbed by the events in Salem. He considered the evidence that was being utilized to determine whether a person was a witch to be quite questionable and stated: "It were better that ten suspected witches should escape than that one innocent person should be condemned. . . . I had rather judge a witch to be an honest woman than judge an honest woman as a witch." On the basis of his own examination of the evidence, he concluded that only two demonstrated what he considered to be valid proof of witchcraft. In contrast, his son, Cotton Mather, was much more convinced of the guilt of the accused.

There were many other indignities suffered by those who were judged guilty of witchcraft. Those who were jailed (or members of their families) were required to pay the jailer for their food and other services, even for the chains that bound them. While in jail the debts of the accused individuals mounted, since they could not work and could not provide the money they were being fined. This resulted in confiscation of their property. Even those who were subsequently acquitted found themselves deeply in debt, to the point where they never regained their original economic status.

Interestingly, those who confessed were not hanged. Often their confessions were forced by a variety of tortures, such as verbal persecution, or hanging by the heels until admission of guilt. Once they expressed remorse and renounced the devil they would be temporarily reprieved. It was those who staunchly maintained their innocence who lost their lives. Interestingly, Tituba was jailed, but not hanged. She was ransomed in May 1693 and probably remained a slave thereafter.

On October 26, 1692, the Massachusetts legislature, at the prodding of Reverend Increase Mather, dictated to the Salem magistrates that they use much more stringent requirements before judging an individual guilty of witchcraft. On October 29, 1692, Governor Phips dismissed the court. This basically brought an end to the trials. For many years thereafter courts and churches declared days of penance and prayer in apology for the injustices perpetrated upon the accused. In January 1696 twelve of the jurors signed a statement of contrition, claiming that they had operated under the influence of the devil. In subsequent years survivors of the accused were granted redress and compensation for their losses, and such compensation continued until as recently as 1957.

In summary, it is important to note that the Salem witchcraft trials took place over a relatively limited period: June 2–September 17, 1692. As early as the time that the trials began there were magistrates and jurors who had serious doubts about the validity of the accusations. By the following year there was widespread remorse among the jurors, days of penance and fasting, and compensation.

All this is in contrast to what is going on today, which makes the Salem witchcraft trials appear like a minor aberration in the development of human sanity.

SIMILARITIES BETWEEN THE LATE-TWENTIETH-CENTURY SEX ABUSE HYSTERIA AND THE SALEM WITCHCRAFT HYSTERIA

In Salem we had a situation in which girls, under the influence of a somewhat primitive woman, engendered what are best referred to as hysterical outbursts. Having no reasonable explanation for this strange phenomenon, the physician attributed the cause to the devil. If one substitutes "sex abuse" for "demonic influence," one brings up to date this twentieth-century rendition of the same phenomenon. Then, as now, doctors have played a role in promulgating the myths. Then, as now, the accused individuals were given speedy trials and subjected to the harshest punishments allowed by law. Although, to the best of my knowledge, no one has received capital punishment for sex abuse, there is no question that the long prison sentences given to many falsely accused are the equivalent. There is no question, also, that there must have been some suicides, death by heart attack, and homicides in association with such false accusations.

Common to the two situations, as well, is the progression of the wave of hysteria. In Salem, the hysteria started in the home of Samuel Parris and rapidly spread throughout Salem town and surrounding communities. In the United States the foci have been a number of communities throughout the country; because our methods of communication today are essentially instantaneous, the spread can be accomplished more quickly and efficiently into ever-widening circles of influence. Common also is the progressive elaboration of the accusations as well as their spread to people at every socioeconomic level. Common also is the notoriety enjoyed by the accusers. Never before had these children enjoyed as much attention and power. As long as they kept up a steady flow of accusations, they continued to enjoy the benefits of their allegations. Those who genuinely recognized that they were fabricating stories (true among some of the Salem accusers) appreciated that public recanting would result in significant embarrassment, possibly punitive measures, and certainly an end to the attention and notoriety. A safer course was to come to believe the accusations and make the fabrications become a delusion. And this similarly has been the fate of many children involved in our present sex abuse hysteria.

It is now almost three centuries since the Salem witch trials. Volumes have been written about it and there are probably more to come. One of the most influential commentators on the trials was Charles W. Upham (1802–1875). He was a citizen of Salem who served also as minister, mayor, and U.S. congressman. In his book, *Salem Witchcraft,* he presents his explanation, which, by today's standards, would be considered a very sensitive psychological analysis of the situation. The quotations here from Upham's book are from the work of M. Mappan, *Witches and Historians: Interpretations of Salem* (1980).

> What are we to think of those persons who commenced and continued the accusations—the 'afflicted children' and their associates?
>
> In some instances and to some extent, the steps they took and the testimony they bore may be explained by referring to the mysterious energies of the imagination, the power of enthusiasm, the influence of sympathy, and the general prevalence of credulity, ignorance, superstition, and fanaticism at the time; and it is not probably, that, when they began, they had any idea of the tremendous length to which they were finally led on.
>
> It was perhaps their original design to gratify a love of notoriety or of mischief by creating a sensation and excitement in their neighborhood, or, at the worst, to wreak their vengeance upon one or two individuals who had offended them. They soon, however, became intoxicated by the terrible success of their imposture, and were swept along by the frenzy they had occasioned. It would be much more congenial with our feelings to believe, that these misguided and wretched

young persons early in the proceedings became themselves victims of the delusion into which they plunged every one else. But we are forbidden to form this charitable judgment by the manifestations of art and contrivance, of deliberate cunning and cool malice, they exhibited to the end. Once or twice they were caught in their own snare; and nothing but the blindness of the bewildered community saved them from disgraceful exposure and well-deserved punishment. They appeared as the prosecutors of every poor creature that was tried, and seemed ready to bear testimony against any one upon whom suspicion might happen to fall. It is dreadful to reflect upon the enormity of their wickedness, if they were conscious of imposture throughout. It seems to transcend the capabilities of human crime. There is, perhaps, a slumbering element in the heart of man that sleeps for ever in the bosom of the innocent and good, and requires the perpetration of a great sin to wake it into action, but which, when once aroused, impels the transgressor onward with increasing momentum, as the descending ball is accelerated in its course. It may be that crime begets an appetite for crime, which, like all other appetites, is not quieted but inflamed by gratification.

I hope the reader will agree with me that this is a remarkable statement, coming from a document published in 1867. Upham tells us that the accusations found a sympathetic audience because of ". . . the general prevalence of credulity, ignorance, superstition, and fanaticism at the time; and it is not probably, that, when they began, they had any idea of the tremendous length to which they were finally led on." Today's children, as well, rely on a population of ignorant and gullible individuals, prone to be superstitious and easily swayed by fanatics.

Upham tells us that these children were motivated by a "love of notoriety or of mischief by creating a sensation and excitement in their neighborhood, or, at the worst, to wreak their vengeance upon one or two individuals who had offended them." These children today too have created "a sensation and excitement" and, in some cases (especially child custody disputes), find the accusations a powerful mechanism of vengeance against those whom they believe (even delusionally so) have offended them.

Upham continues: "They soon, however, became intoxicated by the terrible success of their imposture, and were swept along by the frenzy they had occasioned." The children today have indeed been swept up in the mass hysteria to which they have contributed. Common also is the religious structure in which both events were embedded. In Salem there was the repressive Calvinism of the Puritans; in the United States it is the rising tide of fundamentalism with its condemnation of sexuality.

Upham goes on: "Once or twice they were caught in their own snare; and nothing but the blindness of the bewildered community saved them from disgraceful exposure and well-deserved punishment." Today's children can also rely on the "blindness of the bewildered community" (parents, validators, prosecutors, jurors, and a host of others who are swept up in the hysteria) to "save" them "from disgraceful exposure and well-deserved punishment."

The rest of Upham's quotation devotes itself to the "wickedness" of the children. The "children" involved in the Salem witchcraft accusations were nine years old and older. Because youngsters in the nursery school and day-care center cases are generally in the three-to-four year age level, it is much more difficult to impute conscious hostility ("wickedness") to them. However, in child custody disputes, older children are involved and the term *wickedness* is certainly applicable. I have seen many such cases in which the children react with impunity to the devastation they have visited upon their fathers, with little sense of guilt or remorse over the tragedy they have inflicted upon their family's lives. Elsewhere, Upham tells us:

> At this point, if Mr. Parris, the ministers, and magistrates had done their duty, the mischief might have been stopped. The girls ought to have been rebuked for their dangerous and forbidden sorceries and divinations, their meetings broken up, and all such tamperings with alleged supernaturalism and spiritualism frowned upon. Instead of this, the neighboring ministers were summoned to meet at Mr. Parris's house to witness the extraordinary doings of the girls, and all they did

was to endorse, and pray over, them. Countenance was thus given to their pretensions and the public confidence in the reality of their statements established. Magistrates from the town, church-members, leading people, and people of all sorts, flocked to witness the awful power of Satan, as displayed in the tortures and contortions of the "afflicted children" who became objects of wonder, so far as their feats were regarded, and of pity in view of their agonies and convulsions.

Here we see how the girls, instead of being rebuked and ignored, were surrounded by an army of "ministers . . . magistrates from the town, church members, leading people, and people of all sorts." Replace these individuals with validators, psychologists, prosecutors, lawyers, friends and relatives, newspaper reporters, and television coverage and we see a repetition of the same phenomenon. In both cases the children became "objects of wonder."

Upham continues: "Immediately, the girls were beset by everybody to say who it was that bewitched them." Here, too, we see a direct analogy. Today's sexually abused children are besieged by authorities who demand that they identify their abusers and anyone in sight may be pointed to.

Upham continues:

At the examination of these persons, the girls were first brought before the public, and the awful power in their hands revealed to them. The success with which they acted their parts; the novelty of the scene; the ceremonials of the occasion, the magistrates in their imposing dignity and authority, the trappings of the marshal and his officers, the forms of proceeding,—all which they had never seen before; the notice taken of them; the importance attached to them; invested the affair with a strange fascination in their eyes, and awakened a new class of sentiments and ideas in their minds. A love of distinction and notoriety, and the several passions that are gratified by the expression by others of sympathy, wonder, and admiration, were brought into play. The fact that all eyes were upon them, with the special notice of the magistrates, the entire confidence with which their statements were received, flattered and beguiled them.

The children involved in the sex abuse hysteria exhibit a "love of distinction and notoriety." They enjoy the "entire confidence with which their statements were received." This attention "flattered, and beguiled them."

Upham continues:

A fearful responsibility has been assumed, and they were irretrievably committed to their position. While they adhered to that position, their power was irresistible, and they were sure of the public sympathy and of being cherished by the public favor. If they faltered, they would be the objects of universal execration and the severest penalties of law for the wrongs already done and the falsehoods already sworn to. There was no retracing their steps; and their only safety was in continuing the excitement they had raised. New victims were constantly required to prolong the delusion, fresh fuel to keep up with the conflagration; and they went on to cry out upon others.

These children today become "irretrievably committed to their position." If they falter, they would be "the objects of universal execration and the severest penalties of law for the wrongs already done and the falsehoods already sworn to."

Upham again states:

. . . they were very indifferent as to whom they should accuse. They were willing, as to that matter, to follow the suggestions of others, and availed themselves of all the gossip and slander and unfriendly talk in their families that reached their ears. It was found, that a hint, with a little information as to persons, places, and circumstances, conveyed to them by those who had resentments and grudges to gratify, would be sufficient for the purpose. There is reason to fear, that there were some behind them, giving direction to the accusations, and managing the frightful machinery, all the way through. The persons who were apprehended had, to a considerable extent, been obnoxious, and subject to prejudice, in connection with quarrels and controversies.

The children today are similarly indifferent regarding whom they accuse and they readily follow the "suggestions of others" (such as parents, validators, prosecutors, lawyers, and anyone else who has a vested interest in providing the names of alleged perpetrators). Although the "quarrels and controversies" that existed in Salem in 1692 were certainly different from the "quarrels and controversies" that exist in the United States in the 1980s and 1990s, the principles here are the same. If a divorcing mother wants to "wreak vengeance" on a despised husband, she can easily use her children's allegations of sex abuse to achieve this goal. Hysterical parents who want to stamp out every manifestation of sexuality can use nursery school teachers as the scapegoats for their campaigns. Zealous feminists who want to destroy every man can similarly use innocent children as weapons in their campaign.

Upham continues:

Perpetual conversance with ideas of supernaturalism; daily and nightly communications, whether in the form of conscious imposture or honest delusion, with the spiritual world, continued through a great length of time—as much at least as the exclusive contemplation of any one idea or class of ideas—must be allowed to be unsalutary. Whatever keeps the thoughts wholly apart from the objects of real and natural life, and absorbs them in abstractions, cannot be favorable to the soundness of the faculties or the tone of the mind.

These children today, as well, suffer with psychopathological reactions that are derivative of the obsessive preoccupation with sexuality that their involvement in these cases requires. Not only are they usually subjected to a parade of validators, prosecutors, and lawyers, but hear incessantly and repeatedly in their homes and neighborhoods the details of their plight. This must be "unsalutary" and "cannot be favorable to the soundness of the faculties or the tone of the mind."

Upham again:

Sin in all cases, when considered by a mind that surveys the whole field, is itself insanity. In the case of these accusers, it was so great as to prove, by its very monstrousness, that it had actually subverted their nature and overthrown their reason. They followed their victims to the gallows, and jeered, scoffed, insulted them in their dying hours.

We see the same phenomenon in children today who provide false accusations in custody disputes; they have little or no guilt over the damage they wreak on the lives of their fathers. And watch the McMartin children on television. They too scream and rant at their alleged abusers. Leniency is unacceptable. No punishment is great enough. The primary victims here are those who have been falsely accused. But the children who were allegedly abused are also victims in another sense. They are victims of all the individuals who have been swept up in the parade of hysteria. They are the victims of the validators, the lawyers, the psychologists, the psychiatrists, the prosecutors, and all the others who draw them into the wave of hysteria. And their parents, as well, although they too join forces with the aforementioned parade, are also victims because of their gullibility and, in some cases, their greed (to profit financially through their lawsuits).

One last point of important similarity. The basic tenet of the Salem witchcraft hysteria was that Satan exists and that he exercises his influence through witches who, in turn, could possess innocent victims, such as the children and young women of Salem. And this premise is also held by that segment of today's sex abuse accusers who believe, as well, that Satan exists, that he exercises his will through intermediaries, and that he can indeed possess individuals to perform a wide variety of terrible acts—including sex abuse. In Salem, the local doctor explained the children's symptoms as a derivative of Satan's mischief. And today, there are doctors (psychologists and psychiatrists) and other mental health professionals who also hold such beliefs. Without their credulity, this aspect of the sex abuse hysteria would not have taken hold and joined in with the mainstream of the hysterics who had preceded them by a few years.

THE MAJOR DIFFERENCES BETWEEN THE SALEM WITCH TRIALS AND OUR TWENTIETH-CENTURY SEX ABUSE HYSTERIA

Of course, there are certain points of difference for which Upham's explanation do not invite comparison. First, most of the children in the nursery school and day-care center situations are three to four years of age. The girls who started the Salem witchcraft fiasco were nine and eleven, and others who were "bewitched" were older. Upham considers the conscious fabrication element to be quite important and describes the girls as having developed over the course of the trial "acting such as has seldom been surpassed on the boards of any theatre, high or low, ancient or modern." One cannot attribute such acting skills to the day-care center children. One can, however, ascribe these skills to some of the children I have seen in child custody disputes.

The Salem witch trial tragedy was short lived, with only four months of trial. At this point, our present-day rendition has been going on approximately ten years. Twenty-four people died in Salem. I suspect that there have been many more than 24 deaths associated with the present wave of hysteria; certainly hundreds of lives have been destroyed. Quite early in the Salem proceedings, Judge Nathaniel Saltonstall removed himself because of his recognition that things were getting out of hand. To the best of my knowledge, there have been only isolated examples of voluntary removal by validators, prosecutors, and lawyers because of their awareness that the charges are fabricated and/or delusional. (One of the lawyers in the prosecutor's office in the McMartin case openly expressed disbelief and was promptly dismissed.) Cessation of the trials, which had been accomplished in a relatively short period during the days of the Salem witch trials, is likely to take a much longer time for our present sex abuse hysteria. I believe, however, that more people are "getting wise," but we still have a long way to go. My hope is that judges will become increasingly alerted to the preposterousness of many of the sex abuse allegations that are being made in their courtrooms and be less inclined to "roll" with the hysteria. Here again it is very difficult to assess whether such a change is taking place, but I do believe that judges too are "getting wise" to what is going on here. My hope is that this book will play a role (admittedly small) in reversing the wave of hysteria and will introduce a note of sanity into what may very well be the most widespread and destructive example of mass hysteria in the history of our country.

As I have stated previously, I recognize that the vast majority (probably over 95%) of sex abuse allegations—from *all* situations (especially intrafamilial)—are valid. It is to the small minority—the false accusations (especially in the day-care center and custody dispute situations)—that this book is devoted. I am in full sympathy with those children who have been genuinely victimized by sex abuse. However, children embroiled in false sex abuse allegations are victims in another sense. They are the victims of the parade of parents, "validators," "therapists," prosecutors, and other legal and mental health professionals who use them to serve their own ends. Our sympathies must also go out to these children as well as the adult victims of false sex abuse allegations. My focus here has been on the victims of false sex abuse accusations because they have not been given the sympathy and attention they deserve. It is my hope that this book will serve this purpose and that it will provide guidelines for rectifying and preventing the tragedy of their victimization.

EPILOGUE
SECOND EDITION, NOVEMBER 1992

At the time I wrote this book in 1991, I was not aware of the important role of the *Child Abuse Prevention and Treatment Act* (*Public Law 93-247*) (sometimes referred to as "The Mondale Act") in bringing about the sex-abuse hysteria we are witnessing today. When this legislation was passed by Congress in 1974, child abuse was rarely reported. In fact, its denial and cover-up were widespread. It was Congress's intent to rectify this deplorable situation by providing incentives for states to set up programs for child-abuse research, education, prevention, identification, prosecution, and treatment. Federal funding was made available to match state funding, and this served as an incentive for states to set up such programs. In subsequent years the law was expanded and modified (P.L. 100-294, P.L. 101-126, P.L. 101-226, and P.L. 102-295), especially with regard to the progressive increase in the amount of federal money allocated to the states. There were certain provisions, however, that had to be satisfied in order for a state to qualify for federal monies. Of pertinence to my discussion here is that participating states had to pass legislation that

1. provided immunity from prosecution for all those reporting child abuse and

2. required specific persons (such as health-care professionals, law-enforcement officials, teachers, and school administrators) to report suspected child abuse to the appropriate child protection agency. Such mandated reporting, by necessity, had to be backed up by penalties (usually fines and/or prison sentences) for failure to report. In effect, this provision has made it a criminal offense for such designated persons not to report suspected abuse.

During the next few years all 50 states passed legislation providing for the establishment and funding of the appropriate programs. In addition, funding has been provided to the District of Columbia, the Commonwealth of Puerto Rico, the Virgin Islands of the U.S., Guam, American Samoa, the Marshall Islands, the Commonwealth of the Northern Mariana Islands, and the Trust Territory of the Pacific Islands.

It cannot be denied that those who crafted this legislation were well-meaning, and they cannot be faulted for not having foreseen the widespread grief that has been caused by the Act's implementation by the kinds of misguided and incompetent workers described in this book. One central problem has been that state and federal money is available for the treatment of children who are found to have been abused, but no monies have been specifically allocated for the protection and treatment of those who have been falsely accused and/or children who have suffered psychiatric disturbances because they have been used as vehicles for the promulgation of a false accusation. Accordingly, an evaluator who concludes that abuse has occurred can justify recommending treatment for which state and federal monies will be provided. If the evaluator concludes that no abuse has occurred, there is no route for requesting funding for further evaluation and/or treatment.

In addition, there is a complex network of interaction and interdependence among mental health facilities, child protection services, and investigatory agencies (including police, detectives, and prosecutors). It behooves all working in this network to "cooperate" with one another because the greater the number of referrals, the greater the justification for the requisite funding. Laws mandating the reporting of child abuse and laws providing immunity from prosecution for those reporting abuse ensure an endless stream of referrals for investigators and "validators." All this predictably fuels the sex-abuse hysteria described in this book, hysteria in which an accused individual's Constitutional due-process protections are commonly ignored. These important elements contributing to the hysteria will remain operative unless legislative changes are made at both federal and state levels. Obviously, state-level changes are less likely to be enacted as long as the federal statutes remain in force. It is at the federal level, then, that the changes must be made, especially because of the immunity and mandated reporting clauses, which states cannot rescind without depriving themselves of federal funding.

These are the changes I consider crucial:

1. The federal immunity clause must be dropped. Immunity from prosecution is generally available only to specific groups essential to the functioning of the legal system, e.g., judges and prosecutors. It is incompatible with the basic philosophy of our legal system. Such immunity encourages frivolous and fabricated accusations. I would go further and recommend that states that include the immunity provision should *not* be entitled to federal funding. This change alone would have a formidable effect upon the hysteria we are witnessing today. It would, more than anything else, reduce significantly the flood of false referrals being generated at this time.

2. The clause mandating the reporting of child abuse must be dropped. In practice, it has resulted in the reporting of the most frivolous and absurd accusations by two-and- three-year-olds, vengeful former wives, hysterical mothers of nursery-school children, and severely disturbed women against their elderly fathers. Highly skilled examiners, professionals who are extremely knowledgeable about sex abuse, examiners who know quite well that the accusation is false, are required by law to report the abuse to individuals who they often know to be inexperienced and even incompetent. Yet they face criminal charges if they do not report these accusations.

3. States in which suspected individuals are deprived of Constitutional due-process protections shall not be provided federal funding. In order to ensure the implementation of this require-

ment, states must provide verification that their investigatory and prosecutory procedures provide due-process protections before federal funding is made available.

4. The federal laws now provide funding for child abuse research, education, prevention, identification, prosecution, and treatment. Similar funding should be provided for programs designed to assist those who are falsely accused, as well as children who have been victimized by being used as vehicles for a false accusation. States failing to provide similar funding and facilities for the falsely accused and such victimized children should be deprived of federal funding. Such programs could be combined with existing child-abuse and child-neglect programs.

5. The federal law should require investigatory agencies at all levels to routinely notify and invite for voluntary interview(s) *every* individual accused of child abuse or neglect. (These suspects, of course, must first be informed of their legal rights.) The failure to routinely extend such invitations should deprive the agency of funding.

6. The federal law requires legal representation (a guardian ad litem) for the child victim, but does not require legal representation for the children who are victims of embroilment in false accusations. These children also should be provided with such representation, and the failure to do so should deprive the state of funding.

These proposals are not simply my own. They represent an amalgam of suggestions and recommendations provided by colleagues of mine in both the legal and mental health professions, especially Elizabeth F. Loftus, Ph.D.; Jay Milano, Esq.; Morton Stavis, Esq.; and James S. Wulach, Ph.D., J.D.

In addition to changing the federal law, we need more active backlash by those who have been falsely accused. We need more well-publicized civil lawsuits against incompetent and/or overzealous psychologists, psychiatrists, social workers, child protection workers, "child advocates," police, and detectives whose ineptitude has promulgated a false accusation. I recognize that success in such lawsuits may be difficult, especially in situations in which the vast majority of the defendant's colleagues and peers are operating at the same level of zealotry and incompetence. Furthermore, the falsely accused have to be more active in taking action against lawyers who generate frivolous lawsuits. Moreover, every attempt must be made, through every possible medium, to bring to the attention of the general public the abomination that we are experiencing at this time. I myself have been an active participant in this realm and believe that some headway is being made. The media's thick wall of resistance to even giving consideration to the views of people like myself is starting to erode; however, I still view the public media as resistant to giving reasonable voice, time, and exposure to those like myself who are trying to bring this hysteria to the attention of the public.

These recommendations should be viewed as initial proposals at this time. I recognize that modifications may very well be necessary before they can be implemented. However, to the degree that these recommendations are implemented, to that degree can we hope for some kind of a turnaround in what is clearly one of the greatest waves of hysteria ever to descend upon the United States. If they are not implemented, there is a high likelihood that the hysteria and the victimization of the falsely accused will continue.

. . . As one small candle may light a thousand, so the light here kindled hath shone unto many, yea in some sort to our whole nation.

William Bradford
Governor of the Plymouth Colony, 1621–1656
(Regarding the Mayflower Compact)

REFERENCES

The American Psychiatric Association (1987), *Diagnostic and Statistical Manual, Third Edition-Revised (DSM-III-R)*. Washington, DC: American Psychiatric Association.

Becker, E. (1973), *The Denial of Death*. New York: The Free Press (Macmillan).

Carlson, M. (1990), Six years of trial by torture. In: *Time*, January 29, 1990.

Freud, S. (1905), Three Contributions to the Theory of Sex: II—Infantile Sexuality. In *The Basic Writings of Sigmund Freud*, ed. A. A. Brill, pp. 592-593. New York: Random House, Inc. (The Modern Library), 1938.

——————— (1909), A phobia in a five-year-old boy. In *Collected Papers*, Vol. 3, pp. 149-209. New York: Basic Books, Inc., 1959.

——————— (1930), *Civilization and its Discontents*. London: The Hogarth Press, Ltd., 1951.

Gardner, R. A. (1982), *Family Evaluation in Child Custody Litigation*. Cresskill, New Jersey: Creative Therapeutics.

——————— (1986a), *The Psychotherapeutic Techniques of Richard A. Gardner*. Cresskill, New Jersey: Creative Therapeutics.

——————— (1986b), *Child Custody Litigation: A Guide for Parents and Mental Health Professionals*. Cresskill, New Jersey: Creative Therapeutics.

——————— (1987), *The Parental Alienation Syndrome and the Differentiation Between Fabricated and Genuine Child Sex Abuse*. Cresskill, New Jersey: Creative Therapeutics.

_____ (1988a), Clinical Evaluation of Alleged Sex Abuse. In *Innovations in Clinical Practice: A Source Book,* ed. P. Keller and S. R. Keyman, Vol. VII, pp. 61–76. Sarasota, Florida: Professional Resource Exchange, Inc.

_____ (1988b), *Psychotherapy with Adolescents.* Cresskill, New Jersey: Creative Therapeutics.

_____ (1989a), Differentiating Between Bona Fide and Fabricated Sex Abuse Allegations in Children. In *Journal of the American Academy of Matrimonial Lawyers,* 5:1–25.

_____ (1989b), *Family Evaluation in Child Custody Mediation, Arbitration, and Litigation.* Cresskill, New Jersey: Creative Therapeutics.

Goleman, D. (1988), Lies can point to mental disorders or signal normal growth. *The New York Times,* May 17, 1988, pp. C1, C6.

_____ (1990), Perils seen in warnings about abuse. *The New York Times,* November 21, 1989, p. C11.

Krivacska, J. J. (1989), *Designing Child Sex Abuse Prevention Programs.* Springfield, Illinois: Charles C Thomas, Publisher.

Legrand, R., Wakefield, H., and Underwager, R. (1989), Alleged Behavioral Indicators of Sex Abuse. *Issues in Child Abuse Accusations,* 2(1):1–5.

Lieberman, J. K. (1983), *The Litigious Society.* New York: Basic Books.

Mappan, M. (1980), *Witches and Historians.* Malabar, Florida: Robert E. Krieger Publishing Co.

Milgram, S. (1974), *Obedience to Authority—An Experimental View.* New York: Harper & Row.

Miller, R. (1990), Personal communication.

Mullahy, P. (1970), *Psychoanalysis and Interpersonal Psychiatry.* New York: Jason Aronson, Inc.

Murray, H. (1936), *The Thematic Apperception Test.* New York: The Psychological Corp.

Nathan, D. (1990), The ritual sex abuse hoax. *The Village Voice,* June 12, 1990.

Ravitch, D., and Finn, C. E. (1987), *What Do Our 17-Year-Olds Know?,* New York: Harper & Row.

Richardson, K. W. (1983), *The Salem Witchcraft Trials.* Salem, Massachusetts: Essex Institute.

Thompson, R. (1982), *The Witches of Salem.* London: The Folio Society.

Varendock, J. (1911), Les teroignages d'enfants dans un process retenisant. *Archives of Psychology,* 11:29.

Wakefield, H. and Underwager, R. (1987), *Accusations of Child Sexual Abuse.* Springfield, IL: Charles C Thomas, Publisher.

Author Index

Subject Index

Richard A. Gardner, M.D., a practicing child psychiatrist and adult psychoanalyst, is Clinical Professor of Child Psychiatry at the College of Physicians and Surgeons, Columbia University. He has been a faculty member of the William A. White Psychoanalytic Institute and has served as Visiting Professor of Child Psychiatry at the University of Louvain in Belgium.

Among child therapists Dr. Gardner is recognized as one of the leading innovators in the field. His numerous books, articles, audiotapes, and videotapes (numbering over 250) on various aspects of child psychotherapeutic technique are considered by many therapists to be among the most useful and creative in the literature. Furthermore, he has lectured extensively to mental health and legal professionals, throughout the U.S. and abroad, on a wide variety of topics related to child psychiatry.

Dr. Gardner is certified in psychiatry and child psychiatry by the American Board of Psychiatry and Neurology. He is a Fellow of the American Psychiatric Association, the American Academy of Child and Adolescent Psychiatry, the American Academy of Psychoanalysis, and a member of the American Academy of Psychiatry and the Law. He is listed in *Contemporary Authors, Who's Who in America,* and *Who's Who in the World.*